D0709522

TRUE
RESURRECTION

By the same author
JESUS AND THE RESURRECTION
GOD'S WISDOM IN CHRIST'S CROSS
THE FOUR LAST THINGS
THE TRUE WILDERNESS

Contributed to
OBJECTIONS TO CHRISTIAN BELIEF
SOUNDINGS
THE GOD I WANT

v

TRUE
RESURRECTION

H. A. WILLIAMS

Priest of the Community of the Resurrection

HOLT, RINEHART AND WINSTON

NEW YORK / CHICAGO / SAN FRANCISCO

ISBN: 0-03-091994-0
Library of Congress Catalog Card Number: 72-78108
First printed in the United States in 1972

Printed in the United States of America

ACKNOWLEDGEMENTS

The author and publishers are grateful to the following for their per-
mission to quote copyright material from the sources indicated:

Faber & Faber Ltd, London, and Harcourt Brace Jovanovich Inc., New
York: 'The Dry Salvages', from *Four Quartets* by T. S. Eliot; Faber &
Faber Ltd, London, and Random House Inc., New York: 'His Excel-
lency', from *Collected Shorter Poems 1927–1957* by W. H. Auden;
William Heinemann Ltd, London, and The Macmillan Company,
New York: *Crime and Punishment* and *The Brothers Karamazov* by
Fyodor Dostoevsky, both translated by Constance Garnett; Methuen &
Co. Ltd, London: *The Crown of Life* by G. Wilson Knight; M. B. Yeats
and Macmillan & Co., London, and The Macmillan Company, New
York: 'Supernatural Songs', from *The Collected Poems of W. B. Yeats*
(U.S. Copyright 1934 by The Macmillan Company, renewed 1962 by
Bertha Georgie Yeats).

To the Members & Honorary
Members of the
Church of England Ramblers Association

CONTENTS

PREFACE

THIS book is an attempt to explore my own experience. In writing it I was interested to discover that in some ways my experience has been closer to the tradition of the Eastern Orthodox Church than to that of Western Christianity.

As I said in my essay in *Soundings* and in the introduction to *The True Wilderness*, I have long felt that theological inquiry is basically related to self-awareness and that therefore it involves a process of self-discovery so that, whatever else theology is, it must in some sense be a theology of the self. This view I have found corroborated in the Orthodox tradition. 'Orthodox religious thought lays the utmost emphasis on the image of God in man. Man is "a living theology", and because he is God's icon, he can find God by looking within his own heart, by "returning within himself".'[1]

I have found too among the Eastern fathers an emphasis on unknowing as the inevitable medium of our knowledge of God. Technically this is called the apophatic method, in which a positive statement about God has to be denied in the same breath in which it is affirmed. It has long seemed to me that Western Christianity, for all its talk of analogy or paradox, has felt too much at ease in its assumption that its dogmatic formulations are representationally adequate descriptions of mystery. E. M. Forster's description of it as 'poor little talkative Christianity' is not very wide of the mark.

Most of all, I have always found it impossible to see the world or anybody in it as without God, as though the created order were not in itself God-bearing but were a sort of spiritual vacuum until reclaimed by grace as an almost technical operation. And here it

[1] Timothy Ware, *The Eastern Orthodox Church*, Penguin Books, 1963, p. 225

seems that my experience is more in line with Eastern Orthodoxy, which sees grace in the act of creation itself so that nothing created is without grace. When the operation of grace is restricted to within technically religious limits, religion and even God himself become desperately parochial and deadeningly unreal. Neither Religionless Christianity nor the Death of God speak to me, but I suspect that much of the dynamic behind both is a reaction against this stifling constriction. Of course Western Christianity would in theory deny that God is available only in processed and packaged form. But in practice it has often spoken and acted as if this were the case. It has often given the impression of thinking itself a limited company which has the patent of the fresh air and the sea.

I should add that this book in no way speaks for Eastern Orthodoxy. It is simply that I have found some facets of my experience nearer to the Eastern than to the Western tradition.

I am aware of a debt to Professor L. C. Knights, partly for suggesting some background reading, but much more as a fellow-member of a seminar in Cambridge from whom I learnt how a disciplined imagination in practice functions, however little in this respect I have been able to imitate him. I must also thank Mr T. R. Henn for providing me with a valuable book-list. I am grateful to Dr C. E. Blacker for her account of exorcism among the Buddhist Nichiren sect in Japan; to the late Professor C. D. Broad for information about the evidence available from psychical research; to the Reverend A. M. Allchin for an Eastern Orthodox bibliography. My thanks are also due to Father Eric Simmons, c.r., our Novice Guardian, for his sympathetic understanding when the writing of this book was in progress. And not least I must thank Mr James Mitchell of Mitchell Beazley Ltd for his unfailing and sometimes long-suffering encouragement. Most of all I am aware of my continuing debt to Dr Christopher Scott of Cambridge and London who for many years was the agent to me of a resurrection which at the start seemed impossible because it was inconceivable.

H. A. WILLIAMS
House of the Resurrection, Mirfield

January 1972

CHAPTER ONE

TRUE
RESURRECTION

For Christians Easter is the supreme festival. The churches are decorated with spring flowers. The bells ring. And hymns of triumphant gladness are the order of the day. And there is no hesitation in proclaiming what is being celebrated. Christ is risen! It is a proclamation about mankind, about the world. All that separates and injures and destroys has been overcome by what unites and heals and creates. Death has been swallowed up by life.

It is a magnificently compelling vision – that is, while it lasts. Perhaps for some people it lasts all the time. If so, they are not the sort of people we meet every day, or, with only average luck, even at all. Others feel deeply moved while singing at an Easter service, but soon afterwards find that they are the same people as before and life is as humdrum. Others again find in the Easter celebrations a sort of seasonal ecclesiastical excitement in which they think they ought to join, although they are basically untouched by it. While for others again (the vast majority of people in this country) Easter means nothing whatever. They are unaware of it except as a public holiday. They may have heard of resurrection. If so, they assume it lies outside the area of their experience and concern.

If the vision of Easter is soon lost, or by most people has never been found, that may well be because resurrection has always looked like something in the distance or on the horizon. We can be told about it. But we can have no personal experience of it. When therefore it is affirmed that all that separates and injures and destroys has been overcome by what unites and heals and creates, it may sound like a dream, and people may be as uninterested as they generally are in other people's dreams. Or if they take it seriously, they will want to ask – 'Where does this happen? When does it happen? Can we see and know it for ourselves or can we only be given information about it as about something which belongs to another time and place?'

Resurrection, at least in Western Christendom, has invariably been described as belonging to another time and place. The typical emphasis has been upon the past and future – a past and future with which our connection can only be theoretical, however correct the theory is held to be. So, for example, a book about the resurrection is naturally assumed to be a discussion either about what can be held to have happened in the environs of Jerusalem and Galilee on the third day after Jesus was crucified or about what can be held to be in store for us after our own death. Theories, if they happen to coincide with our own particular areas of interest, can excite the mind. Otherwise they can do nothing. And resurrection, as belonging to the past and future, can only be theoretical. What we know of the past we can know only as information, however well attested we consider it is; and what we know of the future we can know only as speculation, however reasonable we consider the inferences made. When, therefore, a past or future event is described it cannot be something which impinges upon us now with contemporary power.

The past, as past, is dead. We have access to it only by means of the hearsay historians call evidence, and from that evidence we construct a mental picture which at best is no more than the most probable theory of what occurred. This is so even when in the ordinary sense there is no doubt about it at all. Who doubts that Wellington defeated Napoleon at Waterloo? Yet that victory remains no more than a mental construct. We assent to it on the level of theory. We may speculate that Europe would now be a different place had Napoleon instead been the victor. But our reactions to Waterloo are purely cerebral. Like all events of long ago, it has no power to warm or freeze the blood. It raises no living issue and compels us to no fundamental choice. Even if a politician were to use it successfully as the focus of national excitement and aspiration, it would be the contemporary issues which excited and inspired, of which the past event would be no more than a convenient representation. Thought, it has been said, is always a post-mortem. And the past is confined to the boundaries of thought. It is a matter of theory or doctrine, whether it be concerned with what happened at Waterloo in 1815 or with what happened in the environs of Jerusalem and Galilee the third day after Jesus was crucified.

The future more obviously than the past is a matter of theory. We can speculate on what may happen and bring strong arguments to bear in support of our speculations. But as speculation the future remains only a mental product. It has no power to bite us until, as we say, it catches up with us – until, that is, it ceases to be the future and becomes the present. That is so even with regard to a short-term future. How much bite, for instance, had the prophecies of Winston Churchill about the intentions of Nazi Germany until the Second World War was upon us? Or, on a longer term, is even the most devout of Marxists concerned with that withering away of the state which Marx prophesied as the inevitable outcome of the classless society? Or, on the longest view of all, when in medieval Europe the everlasting torments of hell were considered by everybody to be doctrine of indisputable truth, did it make men sin less than they always had done and have done subsequently? Like all theory, the future has no teeth. What does not yet exist cannot be experienced as in any way compelling.

When therefore resurrection is considered in terms of past and future, it is robbed of its impact on the present. That is why for most of the time resurrection means little to us. It is remote and isolated. And that is why for the majority of people it means nothing. Information must be treated as information, speculation as speculation, and both must be assessed accordingly. They cannot be privileged. They demand to be received critically. And, as a matter of contingent historical fact, who can be certain of what happened in Palestine 2,000 years ago, especially when such evidence as we have does not make it at all clear what exactly is supposed to have happened? We cannot be certain when we do not know what we are supposed to be certain about. Or what interest can people be expected to take in fantasies of some life beyond the grave which look as if they are little more than wishful thinking? People do well to be sceptical of beliefs not anchored in present experience, for they invariably belong to the land of compensatory dreams. Scepticism, said Santayana, is the chastity of the intellect. And no age perhaps has been more chaste than our own. We may indeed, in the words of W. H. Auden, be in danger of becoming tight-arsed old maids. But that does not mean that we should expect people to throw chastity completely to the winds and indulge in orgies of extravagant rubbish. Fantasies dissociated from daily life must be rejected if we are not to grow mentally and spiritually soft.

2

At this point I find myself wanting as a Christian to claim that this anchor in daily life is provided by my personal experience here and now of Christ raised from the dead. I say my prayers. I read the Bible. I go to church. I receive the sacraments. And cannot I truly claim that in the course of these activities I have communion now with Christ as a living person?

Most certainly I can. At the same time honesty requires that a number of comments be made.

Reality, to begin with, always comes to us wrapped up in illusion, as Christian writers have been the first to point out. What therefore I consider my experience of Christ raised from the dead cannot be simply or only that. It will also contain projections from my own unconscious wishes and thus be partly a private fantasy. Christians are not exempt from man's habitual tendency to make gods in his own image. There is also another even more important fact which I cannot ignore. Maybe that after a painfully long and perplexing journey I do discover something of the reality of the living Christ. But what I then find is remarkably similar and often identical with what has been found by unwearied seekers who either started as Jews, Buddhists, Vedantists, or Moslems, or who have found this mysterious reality without having hung any religious label round their necks. That indeed is what I should expect if I equate Christ with the Eternal Word which enlighteneth every man. But I find that I and my fellow Christians do not always expect it. On the contrary, I find it often causes suspicion and anxiety. Intellectual guns are often primed and shot in passion to demonstrate that the Eternal Word is the exclusive possession of Christians. And I am left wondering whether this anxiety to prove exclusive possession does not suggest a confusion of the Eternal Word with a cult-idol (for it is idols which need protecting, not God) – a confusion to which, I suspect, the devotees of all religions are liable.

Hence, although I want to offer my experience of Christ in prayer and sacrament as the anchor in the present of my belief in resurrection, I am doubtful whether the argument is wholly legitimate and surmise that this may be the reason why, as far as most people are concerned, such so-called witness is totally ineffective. The gem of reality is too wrapped up in the coloured paper of illusion. If what in fact I offer to people is to a large extent my own particular cult-idol – even if it is an idol I share with the majority of churchgoers – then it can be no surprise that it means little or nothing to them. For cult-idols are a matter of temperament and inclination, and there is no reason why the cult-idol which attracts me should attract others. They may be immune to its charms just as they may have no eye for painting or no head for figures. Nor will it be much good my delivering myself a lecture on the fatal inadequacy of private opinion and the strength of the collective opinion of the innumerable company of believers, since a similar innumerable company has appreciated painting and enjoyed doing their accounts. 'I am just not one of them,' the rejoinder will be.

What makes me even more certain that our Christian experience of what we call the living Christ is at least partly an attachment to a cult-idol is our evident immunity from the threatening glory of resurrection. If, as Christians are supposed to believe, Christ *is* the resurrection, it is strange that life for us invariably means business as usual, especially the business we transact with ourselves. Christ's métier is generally considered to be the preservation of the status quo; in individuals a personal psychic status quo and in the church an institutional status quo, provided that in each case there is a respectable measure of reform, in the individual mostly moral and in the church mostly administrative. There is little sign of the ultimate challenge of Jesus – 'Destroy this temple and in three days I will raise it up.' Indeed our main concern is to preserve the fabric – what we like to call our own mental and spiritual health, and the well-being of the church.

But then the advantage of idols, as second-Isaiah perceived, is that they cannot do anything. They thus leave us free to continue as before. And if our cult-idol inconveniently called himself the resurrection, we have insulated ourselves against this threat by pushing resurrection safely out of the present into the past and future. Christ was the resurrection and he will be. That is how we have allayed our fears. So we can eat, drink, and be, if not merry, at least reasonably comfortable, even when we call the fare provided God's holy food. And if anything, like a *Panorama* programme for instance, suggests that we have died and need resurrection now, we rush to the defence of our cult-idol and its religious clutter as if the Eternal Word could be threatened, even by the BBC. It is a neat trick (all the neater for being unconsciously done) this banishing of resurrection to past and future. It saves us from a lot of reality and delivers us from a great deal of fear. It has, in short, the advantage of safeguarding us from life.

3

Yet there is another side to the picture. Without this other side we could have no hope. We should remain permanently the slaves of our cult-idol. But in the mercy of God it is always possible for the coloured paper of illusion to be unwrapped enough to reveal the gem of reality it has so far hidden. The Eternal Word can begin to be revealed in the features of the cult-idol. Error can be the mediator of truth. Darkness can be the vehicle of light. And this in itself is an experience of resurrection now, of resurrection and of the death which must precede it. The death in this case is a death to familiar and childish certainties. The resurrection consists in our being raised up to a first and no doubt fleeting glance of unmanageable mystery. If religions, or at least the great five or six, do not peter out, can it be because they carry within them the possibility of revealing the Eternal Word to those who have ears to hear? And those who do hear cease to make exclusive jingoist claims for the particular illusions which for them have conveyed the reality. More and more they are compelled to acknowledge that the reality can be found along many and various roads and not least by people who follow no established road at all but cut their own path as they go. The way, the truth, and the life lie on the other side beyond the destruction of the temple. That for many is the most painful death they have to die. It was a death which Jesus accepted. He died upon the cross crying, 'My God, my God, why hast thou forsaken me?' We cannot tell the full significance of that cry. But at least it must mean that Jesus surrendered his role or identity as the teacher who brought to men good news from God, the man certain of his vocation as messiah, the figure in whom God's truth was ultimately revealed. In that loud and exceeding bitter cry such claims and certainties were cast aside and given up in a death which preceded the moment of his dying physically. And it was because of this renunciation that he was given a name which is above every name. 'Destroy this temple' – the temple was himself and all he was, his beliefs, his hopes, his certainties, his identity as the one sent from the Father. But if the temple was destroyed, it was only that it might be raised indestructible. It was in the surrender of all he was that he became transparent to the Eternal Word in whom all things in heaven and on earth are to be gathered into one.

In the surrender of the cross Jesus is shown to be the opposite of a cult-idol. Cult-idols are neurotically concerned to preserve each its own exclusive rights, 'for they that make them are like unto them'. Jesus abandons all his claims in the stripping naked of Calvary. And it is precisely because of his nakedness that he is able to reveal the Eternal Word. For the Eternal Word is not in competition with other claimants. He is not in this sense a successful Pretender. And so he can make himself heard in all languages by all races, and his voice can come to be recognized speaking by means of all religions or none.

4

But how, then, can we know that we have heard the Eternal Word?

It is by the fact that to hear him is always to be raised from the dead. Where there is resurrection, there the Eternal Word has spoken. And where there is no resurrection, there the voice of the Eternal Word has not yet penetrated, be men never so earnest, be they never so religious.

But what, then, is resurrection? If it happens to us now, how are we to identify it? How are we to know that it has occurred or is occurring? What are the signs of its coming?

What we hanker after is a sign from heaven which cannot be spoken against, an experience in which we are lifted out of the tears and sweat and dirt of our humanity into a serene empyrean where the gritty quality of our ordinary daily life is left far behind and can be forgotten. But resurrection as a present miracle does not deliver us from the unevenness and turmoil and fragmentariness of being human. The miracle is to be found precisely within the ordinary round and daily routine of our lives. Resurrection occurs to us as we are, and its coming is generally quiet and unobtrusive and we may hardly be aware of its creative power. It is often only later that we realize that in some way or other we have been raised to newness of life, and so have heard the voice of the Eternal Word.

5

To give some concrete examples:

An artist, at first only painfully aware of an utter emptiness and impotence, finds his imagination gradually stirred into life and discovers a vision which takes control of him and which he feels not only able but compelled to express. That is resurrection. Or a scholar or scientist as he pursues his research finds a favourite theory breaking up in his hands. He is left with no home in which to house the quantities of evidence he has collected. Then a new more adequate theory gradually takes shape in his mind which makes him more at home with his material even than he was before. That is resurrection. Or a married couple find their old relationship, once rich and fulfilling, slowly drying up into no more than an external observance to the point where it seemed impossible that these dry bones should ever live again. Then a new relationship emerges, less superficially high powered and less greedy than the old one, but deeper, more stable, more satisfying, with a new quality of life which is inexhaustible because it does not depend on the constant recharging of emotional batteries. That is resurrection. Or an individual finds life less and less rewarding, not on its public and professional side, where he may be very successful, but in its failing to bring in an adequate degree of personal fulfilment. He seems to get less and less of what he wants and values most, although he does not know what it is. He feels intolerably isolated on a rubbish dump he cannot get off. He has identified what he is with a limited and false portrait of himself which he was successfully sold by an unconscious conviction that limitation means safety. But the supposed claims of safety are emptying his life of content. Yet in the midst of his despair he discovers a broader basis on which to establish himself, and, in spite of the threatening danger, fills up more of his own space, lets himself in for more of what he is, and thus finds a richer more satisfying life. That is resurrection. Or suffering, a severe illness, or a catastrophe like the premature death of someone deeply loved, such suffering is always destructive. People, we say, are never the same again. Sometimes they shrivel up and atrophy. But appearances here can be deceptive. Under the devastation of their ordeal which leaves its deep and permanent traces, one can be aware that they are in touch with a new dimension of reality. They have somehow penetrated to the centre of the universe. They are greater people. They are more deeply alive. That is resurrection. Or, on a lighter but by no means insignificant level, the prisoner of irritating or confining circumstances, the man who slips on one of the many kinds of banana skin, the man whose great expectations are belied, the man who is tied to triviality, realizes the humour of his situation, and by his laughter shows that he has risen above what cabins and confines him because he can relish the joke at his own expense. That is resurrection.

Resurrection is always a mystery. It is always a miracle. It is always the creative act of the Eternal Word. Because that Word is spoken now in the present in terms of what we call the common circumstances of life, there can be nobody who at some time or other has not thus been raised from the dead. But more often than not our eyes are holden and we do not know it. We do not recognize resurrection when it comes to us. The presence of the Eternal Word is unnoticed, and evidenced only in the new life made available; just as at Cana of Galilee the guests enjoyed the good wine but did not know whence it was.

6

The aim of this book is to explore how and when in the course of our lives we are raised from the dead, the occasions when the power of resurrection has been brought to bear upon us. Where do we meet that Eternal Word who *is* the resurrection and the life? In what guises does he appear? In what media does he speak? Do we, like the two disciples on their journey to Emmaus, walk with him in the way, but, unlike them, fail in the end to perceive who he is?

Because he is the creative Word, his presence makes us what we are. It creates and establishes our personal identity. Who and what, then, am I? I assume I am body and mind. How far, then, as body and mind, am I fully all there? How far as body and mind am I dead? And how far as body and mind have I been raised from the dead? What does it consist in, this being fully alive as body and mind? It means being a person, and being a person is resurrection.

What does a person exist to do? A person exists to be the agent of creative goodness. When we thus create goodness we are both ourselves raised from the dead and also the agents to others of resurrection. For genuine goodness always brings life. In the last resort ethics can only be resurrection.

But life is suffering as well as doing. And suffering is death-dealing. How can what is death-dealing be transformed into what is life-giving? How, in our suffering, can we be raised from the dead?

When we begin to recognize the power of resurrection present in the ordinary gritty routine of our daily lives, then we shall see for ourselves that all that separates and injures and destroys is being overcome by what unites and heals and creates. We shall no longer have to ask where and when this happens, for we shall have first-hand experience of it as we live as ordinary folk in the ordinary world.

But what, then, of resurrection as future, of resurrection as our entry into the life of the world to come?

If we have been aware of resurrection in this life, then, and only then, shall we be able or ready to receive the hope of final resurrection after physical death. Resurrection as our final and ultimate future can be known only by those who perceive resurrection with us now encompassing all we are and do. For only then will it be recognized as a country we have already entered and in whose light and warmth we have already lived.

CHAPTER TWO

RESURRECTION & THE BODY

I

A PERSON's body is obviously of primary concern to him. It is as body that I am most immediately aware of myself, and it is to the service of myself as body that my strongest and most elementary instincts are directed. If, therefore, resurrection is a present experience, it must be (among other things) a bodily experience. It is my physical make-up which is raised from the dead.

Seeing, however, that I am still physically alive, how can my body be dead? And while my heart continues to beat and blood to flow through my veins, how can my body be raised from the dead?

Theoretically formulated these are nonsense riddles of a totally unprofitable kind. The appeal must be to experience. But to describe experience requires a background in terms of which to set it out. For me that background is provided by what Christians have believed about the resurrection of the body. Christians have thought of that resurrection as exclusively future – belonging to a life *after* this one. But perhaps what Christians have believed about the future resurrection of the body in an after-life may be a means of setting out the *present* experience of the body's resurrection in this one. If so, it will be worth stopping for a few moments to remind ourselves of what Christians have traditionally meant by the future resurrection of the body. Formal theology may here be a necessary preliminary.

2

The original Latin version of the creed spoke of the resurrection not of the body but of the flesh. This future event of the resurrection of the flesh was for centuries taken quite literally by Christian writers. On the Last Day God would exercise his omnipotent power to reassemble the scattered dust and bones laid in the grave and raise up these reassembled physical particles to endless life. Hence the veneration of relics and the initial objection among many Christians to cremation. Bones had an eternal future as well as a temporary past. This literalistic view, however, was open to the criticism that it contradicted the clear words of St Paul that 'flesh and blood cannot inherit the kingdom of God'.[1] And it was partly to meet this criticism that we may suppose that in the first English Prayer Book published in the sixteenth century the resurrection of the flesh was changed into the resurrection of the body.

St Paul, it has been widely assumed, did not hold what is described as the grossly materialistic view of our future resurrection – that is, he did not subscribe to a view considered axiomatically to be undesirable and therefore superstitious. In fact, however, St Paul on this point is by no means unambiguous. Certainly he denied the resurrection of the flesh. But he also affirmed it. His contention was that the flesh and blood of our physical body as we know it now cannot inherit the kingdom of God. But our future eternal state was not to be bodiless. The physical body as we know it now was not so much to be eliminated as to suffer a sea-change into something he could describe only as a spiritual body. That, of course, was not meant as an empirical description. What he called a spiritual body was not a matter of observation. The term spiritual body was the symbol for a paradox. The body raised at the Last Day would be both identical with our present bodies and at the same time different from them. There would be both continuity with our bodies now and also discontinuity. As an analogy St Paul uses the seed sown by a farmer in the ground. The wheat seed produces wheat and not some other crop. But the harvest is no mere recovery of the seed sown. What is harvested is something new, the result of God's creative action. God has raised the bare wheat seed and given it a new body, but the new body is appropriate to the old and thus in a real sense is related to it. Barley, for instance, does not grow from a wheat seed. The relation therefore between seedtime and harvest is one of both identity and difference. So it will be, concludes St Paul, at the resurrection of the dead. What is sown will be reaped. But it will not be the bare recovery of what

[1] 1 Corinthians 15:50.

is buried. God's creative power will raise up something new – 'It is sown a physical body, it is raised a spiritual body.'[2]

It will be seen that the original form of the creed – the resurrection of the flesh – is not so out of line with St Paul's view as has come to be taken for granted. In the paradox identity-difference, continuity-discontinuity, we have come to lay all the emphasis on the difference and discontinuity, and have forgotten St Paul's equal emphasis on the identity and continuity.

This double emphasis is found again when St Paul talks of the return of Christ in glory. When he wrote 1 Corinthians, St Paul expected this return in the near future, at least some time before all contemporary Christians had died. And when that return occurred, St Paul thought, those still living would not so much lose their physical identity as find it changed into something imperishable: 'We shall not all sleep [in death], but we shall all be changed.'[3] And this change is not described as the abandonment or disappearance of the perishable and the mortal, but as the putting on by the perishable of what is imperishable and the putting on by the mortal of what is immortal.[4] The image of one thing putting on another – of something putting on its opposite – the perishable the imperishable and the mortal the immortal – is as good an image as any for that continuity in discontinuity and identity in difference which marks St Paul's view of our future resurrection. To say therefore that the flesh, in the sense of the physical, is simply eliminated is to ignore one side of the Pauline view. For St Paul it is the flesh as we experience it now in this present age which cannot inherit the kingdom of God. But as well as living in this present age we also, according to St Paul, live now in the age to come. We are now risen with Christ[5] and our citizenship is already in heaven.[6]

St Paul's view that the physical body will not just be abandoned is further corroborated by hints he gives about the destiny of the material universe. It is not to be scrapped as of no permanent significance. For it is in Christ that all things exist,[7] and God's plan

[2] 1 Corinthians 15:44. [3] 1 Corinthians 15:51.
[4] 1 Corinthians 15:53. [5] Colossians 3:1.
[6] Philippians 3:20. [7] 1 Corinthians 8:6.

for the fullness of time is 'to unite all things in Christ, things in heaven and things on earth'.[8] In one passage[9] St Paul describes the whole order of creation as under the dominion of *mataiotes* – the word means vanity, emptiness, unreality, illusion, purposelessness (the Revised Standard Version translates the word 'futility'; the New English Bible translates 'frustration'). Certainly St Paul sees no permanent place in God's plan for the material universe as emptiness or illusion. But the passage speaks of a change or transformation of the material universe so that it is no longer in bondage to perishableness and decay but attains the glorious liberty of God's own children. It is the theme of the perishable putting on the imperishable and the mortal putting on the immortal now widened to include not only individual human beings of flesh and blood but the whole material order. Emptiness or illusion is not, so to speak, the inherent characteristic of matter. It is matter subject to some sort of spell or alienation from which it is God's purpose to deliver it, so that it may share his glory.

3

We are in fact not far here from the religions or philosophies of the East which are generally regarded (by Christians) as in radical contradiction to Christianity on this point. For the maya or illusion which is described as the nature both of personal identity and of the material world belongs to the false estimate of them entertained by the intellect-bound mind. It is the fantasies of itself and the world entertained by the closed-up ego which must be found out as illusion. But once one has died to that false closed-up identity, one obtains the enlightenment to see the self and the universe as divine play – a characteristically eastern view. And this is not so very different from seeing them as divine glory, so long as we understand that this is not a matter of theory or doctrine but of living experience. It is by being part of the Divine Comedy that we come to know it, not by studying and comparing various

[8] Ephesians 1:10.   [9] Romans 8:19, 20.

attempts at programme notes. Here, as so often, 'we do not need theories' but 'the experience which is the source of the theory'.[10]

But the appeal to experience plunges us immediately into the present.

4

What then is the experience which has led us to regard the resurrection of the flesh as 'grossly materialistic' in a pejorative sense, i.e. as totally undesirable?

It is the same experience which has led us to push resurrection itself out of the present safely into the future. It is the experience of fear. Primarily it is of fear full stop. But the free-floating fear must find an object and the object is found in what is closest at hand – in myself as flesh and blood, in myself as body. The body, after all, is vulnerable. At any moment it may be injured or destroyed. And what will physical passions do if given half a chance? Because we are afraid of our bodies we have constructed a theory which dissociates the body from the essential man. We have divided mind from matter and have made matter seem alien from what we consider our true selves. Fear is the experience at the source of all dualistic theories about man. The theories reinforce the fear and the reinforced fear in its turn seems to confirm the theories. Hence the staying power of the dualistic estimate of man. It maintains its influence in practice even when it is held to have been theoretically disproved. Analytical logic is powerless to exorcize the demon of fear. So the division of mind and matter continues to be held at some level of consciousness. What are its consequences?

If I divide myself into two distinguishable entities – mind and matter and soul and body I will begin to ask which of the two is in control.

For Plato and the Greeks there was no question which of the two *should* be in control. Mind should be the master and matter

---

[10] R. D. Laing, *The Politics of Experience and the Bird of Paradise*, Penguin Books, 1967, p. 15.

the slave. The intrinsic man consisted of his rational faculties. His body was little more than an unfortunate accident. For the time being his rational faculties, the human spirit, were imprisoned in a tomb of flesh. A wise man, understanding this, would see to it that the flesh and the passions which arose from it were given no degree whatever of autonomy. By the strictness of its control over the body the human spirit could keep itself free from the body's contamination. Reason, not passion, must be in charge. Of course, this did not always happen. In practice the voice of reason was often overpowered by the strength of a man's bodily passions. But in either case the human person was always divided into two – the controller and the controlled, the master and the slave, whichever role man's reason or his body assumed in any particular case.

This dualism was reforged in the seventeenth century by Descartes. Descartes, starting again from the beginning, asked of what he could be absolutely certain and gave himself the famous answer, 'I think, therefore I am.' From this axiom he proceeded to divide reality into mind and extension or spirit and matter. He did not successfully explain the interaction between the two. But our concern here is that he reinforced the general climate of opinion in terms of which a particular view of man came to be taken for granted. In man, it was assumed, mind and matter, spirit and body, were combined. But this was not a marriage between partners. The real man was his mind. His body was no more than a machine directed and driven by his mind. It is interesting to see how this view lingered in medical practice. Until fairly recently medical practitioners considered themselves concerned with man's body as a machine independent of his mind or state of consciousness. It was assumed that the wheels of the body could be oiled and repaired by drugs or surgery, that the machine could be serviced, without any account being taken of its driver. And this was called scientific medicine as opposed to all forms of witch-doctory. Naturally the patient was only too keen to assume that it was the motor-car which was at fault, not himself as driver. This legacy of Descartes meant that, as with Plato and the Greeks, there was in man the controller and the con-

trolled, thought of no longer so much as master and slave as man and machine. Machines have no autonomy. Within the limits of their mechanical structure they exist to do their owner's bidding.

It makes no difference that this dualistic view of man has been exploded by more recent philosophers. What confronts us is not the technical skill of expert philosophers but a general background of unconscious assumption about human nature which, as we saw, can in practice be entertained even by those who have the expertise to explode it in theory. The dualistic view of man as controller and controlled has a very long history and it dies extremely hard because the continuing experience of fear keeps it alive. There can be nobody in our western culture who does not catch himself out assuming it, while for most of us it is axiomatic. 'Control yourself. Pull yourself together,' we say, without stopping to consider who or what it is that pulls and who or what it is that is pulled.

Even Freud's assumptions about man were basically dualistic. Freud did not of course assume that man had a body and a soul or that he was half mortal and half immortal. He explored the biological urges which are repressed in the subconscious and he saw that these urges, for all their repression, none the less exercised their strong if secret influence upon conscious thought and behaviour. He understood that if these biological urges were too excessively or extensively repressed the result was trouble for the individual – illness or catastrophe. But he had no doubt that the conscious mind must be man's master, and he considered a certain considerable degree of repression – the locking up in the dark room of the subconscious of a great deal of instinctive energy – as the price man had to pay for civilization. Freud sometimes wondered whether, after all, civilization was worth it. For the monster imprisoned in the subconscious not only had ways of making his presence uncomfortably felt all the time, but on occasion would break out of his prison altogether and indulge in an orgy of sadistic rage. In such a view the old dualism persists in a new form. Man is still the controller and the controlled. What Freud did was to suggest a modified *modus vivendi* between them in which the controlled (our instinctual life) should be allowed a certain degree

of self-government by being partly, but only partly, taken into consciousness. The dynamic of instinct was for the most part still to continue repressed permanently in the subconscious.

5

This division of man into controller and controlled, having been a central feature of our cultural environment since the time of Plato at least and being fed by our continuing fear, provides us with the eyes with which we look at ourselves. It has become second nature to us and it is difficult for us to see in any other way. Yet western man was provided with an alternative which he failed to take up. This was the Hebrew-Jewish tradition as found in the Old Testament. Here not only was matter good because created by God, but man, far from being a soul or spirit incarcerated in a body, was a body to which God had given life. In this view the body was the man, and the psychic functions were thought of as distributed among the various physical organs. The hand in the literal sense had its own cunning, for instance. The bowels literally were the locus of compassion. In such a view the death of the body was the death of the whole man. Hence life after death had to be thought of not in terms of some sort of personal survival but in terms of the resurrection of the body from the grave. The experience of fear was by no means absent, but it was projected outwards on to Jehovah, who knew everything and punished every transgression, rather than in the direction of the self as body.

The Hebrew-Jewish tradition was arrested in its influence by the conquests of Alexander the Great (356–323 B.C.). Since that time Jewish thought became infiltrated with Greek ideas, and the dualistic view of man began to be found in Jewish writing, such as the so-called Wisdom of Solomon (about 100 B.C.) in our Apocrypha.

St Paul's view in this connection is interesting. Fundamentally his concept of man is the unmodified Hebrew-Jewish one. Man is a single totality, a being whose one single created nature stands before God. Hence St Paul's refusal to countenance the idea of

man's body being simply eliminated at the Last Day, and also his conviction that the whole material universe had its place in the divine scheme. It is therefore natural for St Paul to exhort the Christians in Rome to offer their bodies to God as a living sacrifice, their spiritual worship, where 'body' obviously means everything they are – i.e. themselves.[11] (Later church prayers spoke of offering 'our souls and bodies as a living sacrifice'.) But St Paul in this matter is by no means always consistent, and the dualism of spirit and matter, controller and controlled, frequently appears as well. It was as if, as well as the fear of the Lord, there had been superimposed upon it at the same time the fear of the physical. So flesh on one side and mind or spirit on the other can be described as warring opposites: 'I serve the law of God with my mind, but with the flesh I serve the law of sin.'[12] The deeds of the body are to be done to death,[13] or we are to do to death what is earthly in us.[14] And in a vivid piece of autobiography St Paul says of himself: 'I pommel my body and subdue it.'[15] Whatever may be considered his deepest or most fundamental view of man, St Paul certainly did his share of riveting the dualistic view upon the mind of Christendom. The older pre-Greek Hebrew-Jewish view of man hardly had a chance.

6

We are left then firmly if unknowingly enslaved to a view of ourselves in which we are divided into two. I am on the one hand my mind and on the other hand my body. I am on the one hand spirit and on the other hand flesh. Or in Freudian terminology, I am on the one hand ego (the controlling principle) and on the other hand id (my biological instincts). And since as well as the duality I am also one person, the two opposites have to fit together in some sort of relation. This relation, unconsciously assumed, will form a status quo in which I shall feel myself totally invested. It will be my way of dealing with my experience of fear

[11] Romans 12:1.   [12] Romans 7:25.   [13] Romans 8:13.
[14] Colossians 3:5.   [15] I Corinthians 9:27.

and I shall uncompromisingly resist any attempt to destroy and replace it.

The structure of this status quo is inevitable. Once I assume the division between mind and matter, spirit and body, ego and id, then of necessity mind, spirit, ego, must be in control and matter, body, id, must be under control. To the question as set any other answer would be nonsense. In my own view of myself therefore the relation between the two selves in my one person must be that of master and servant. The mind or spirit with its power to think and organize must be the master and the body with its physical appetites must be the servant.

7

The trouble with servants, however, is that they seldom know their place. Jack invariably regards himself as good as his master. Just as boys will be boys so servants will be insolent – if, that is, they are ever given the opportunity. So the obvious strategy is to see that the opportunity never arises. If servants are not to have ideas above their station, then they must always be kept under with a firm hand. The more they show signs of insubordination the more must they be suppressed. And since people who are always kept under inevitably feel rebellious, the safest solution is to reduce servants to the status of slaves. For slaves are not people in their own right with their own natural claims. They are simply the property of their owners. If they are to work efficiently they must of course be kept reasonably healthy with adequate food and shelter and so on, just as machines must be stoked and oiled and protected from the weather. But that is all. For what are slaves except machines whose only *raison d'être* is to perform the functions allotted to them by their owners?

It is to a comparable status that the body is reduced when the dualistic assumption about man leads to the body's being distinguished sharply from the mind and being put firmly under the mind's control. In such a set-up the body cannot survive as a servant, for a servant as a fellow-citizen will press his claims to basic equality, and then what will happen to the status quo?

Clearly, apart from its needs for food and shelter, the body must be stripped of its claims to autonomy and be treated as a slave or a machine which is at the disposal of its owner to use as he thinks fit. It must be stressed again that this is not the considered conclusion of any philosophical, theological, or scientific investigation. It is not the result of any sort of conscious reflection. It is an inherited assumption, an attempted answer to the experience of fear, which is taken for granted and which shows itself not as any formulated belief but as the way in which I inevitably set about the business of living, what I assume is the natural way. And even if in the sphere of my particular competence I hold this assumption to be philosophically, theologically, or scientifically false, I shall probably still continue to pay it homage in my actual dealings with people, especially myself, in the practical conduct of life.

As slave or machine the body is dead. Suitably conditioned it will of course function as a machine, sometimes very efficiently. But it has nothing of what could be called life, for it is no more than somebody else's chattel. It can have no wishes and make no claims beyond those of mere self-preservation. When the body as slave-machine functions efficiently and obediently it can be forgotten like a dead man out of mind. When the mechanism runs faultily or shows signs of wearing out I wish I could get rid of it and get a new one as I would like to sell my old car for a more up-to-date model. Or I can grow tired of my body as a man grows tired of his possessions, wishing I could find freedom by disposing of it – 'O that this too too solid flesh would melt, thaw, and resolve itself into a dew.' I may feel an unwilling prisoner in this muddy vesture of decay.

It will be seen that for all its movement the body has been done to death. As its master I have denied it the right to live except as a slave-machine. It is an object, a thing, like the clothes I wear and the car I drive.

8

Since Christians hold a theological theory about the body, that it is good because made by God and that it can, in St Paul's words, become a temple of the Holy Spirit,[16] it might be supposed that they would not allow it to be killed off, that *their* bodies at least would not be dead. But that Christians do none the less regard their body as an object or chattel which (under God) they own can be shown by a very simple test. Let us suppose that in church one Sunday morning the lesson is taken from words of St Paul already quoted: 'I appeal to you therefore, brethren . . . to present your bodies as a living sacrifice, holy and acceptable to God, which is your spiritual worship.'[17] What particular prospect does response to this exhortation conjure up? Does it conjure up the prospect of physical pleasure, physical joy, not to mention physical ecstasy of the kind a lover has when he holds his beloved in his arms? Not at all. The prospect conjured up is the dreary duty of controlling the body, or if the body is recalcitrant of forcing it, negatively, not to do this, that, or the other, and positively to energize itself in the performance of this or the other kind of good works. But whether understood negatively or positively the exhortation is taken automatically as a call to the joyless task of disciplining the body and oppressing it by imposing upon it an alien will, treating it in short as a dead object to be pushed around. This inevitable reaction to St Paul's injunction shows the Christian (whatever fancy theological notions he may have in his brain) sharing the common assumption of western culture that the body is or should be a slave-machine with no life of its own.

9

But just as it is often true of servants that they do not know their place, so it can also be true of the dead that they won't lie down. When somebody who is safely dead and buried makes his presence felt in a ghostly way, the result, to say the least, is disturbing. And this, as Freud pointed out, is precisely the sort of way my dead body continues to exercise its power. Its acceptance of the role of passive object is at best grudging, and it absolutely refuses to be killed off entirely. For all its having been reduced to a serviceable machine, it is always lurking somewhere in the background

[16] I Corinthians 6:19.   [17] Romans 12:1.

ready to give trouble as occasion arises. My body, for instance, may make it difficult for me to pursue what I consider the rational line and force me to implement its own plans instead. I may be driven by passion at the expense of reason – 'Ever till now, when men were fond I smiled and wondered how.' Or my reason may prevail, and my body take its revenge in subtle ways not easy to identify. I may become the victim of some sort of nervous disability or mysterious illness like Elizabeth Barrett before Robert Browning rescued her. Or I may simply never feel really well. By now most doctors have ceased to regard the body as no more than a machine and agree that what the majority of their patients suffer from is what is technically known as conversion hysteria, i.e. the conversion of psychic distress into a physical symptom. As mind, I deny my body's life and keep it like a caged animal to whose howls I have made myself deaf. The pain of that captivity can therefore find expression only in ways which I am prepared to recognize – which means what I consider an above-board physical symptom, a pain in the chest or a tendency to feel faint. It is admitted that some diseases like stomach ulcers and in many cases cancer are what are called stress diseases. They are the wounds caused by the fight between the body's life and the imposed will of the conscious 'rational' personality. But my oppressed body may not cause physical illness. It may simply make me feel that life is empty and ultimately meaningless, the body I have done to death spreading the influence of its deathliness to other areas of my being.

The trouble with killing off the body is that in killing you do not exterminate it so much as consign it to hell. For hell consists of the dead who cannot accept their death. 'Hell is the place of the undead.'[18] Hence the continuation of the body's ghostly influence.

10

An attractively simple answer to this situation is to allow the life of the body to have its head. In so far as practical social circumstances permit, let the passions have as free a play as possible.

[18] Herbert McCabe, O.P., *The New Creation*, Sheed & Ward, 1964, p. 188.

Cease to be conventional and give way to the body's demands. Spend your nights on the tiles. But this easy solution is unfortunately a fallacy and does not work. A slave has to be educated for freedom. He does not become a free man merely in virtue of his master's temporarily renouncing his claims upon him. He will still have the mentality of a slave and it will be as a slave that he will throw away his opportunities of freedom. In other words, the oppression of the body has made it subject to compulsions of various kinds, and the last thing the satisfaction of a compulsion does is to satisfy. All it can do is to afford a little momentary relief, after which it has to be done again – and again and again. It is no doubt healthy for the slave to see that his master can be ignored if only for a short time. In this way it is possible for a night on the tiles to be the beginning of freedom. But what is thus begun often does not develop into anything positive, because the compulsions of instinct merely replace the compulsions of reason. In consequence the body does not find the satisfaction it longs for, and is like somebody who is always on the make and never makes it. The most obvious example is Don Juan whose successes with women never bring him any sense of having succeeded, so that he must try once more. 'Ringing the changes on modes of *getting pleasure* disguises boredom, but it does not restore life. Sex, in such circumstances, is less and less a form of communication and more and more a diversion.'[19] Diversions are salutary in so far as they temporarily relieve tension, but they can never be the bread of life. In any case some of the instincts of the body as an oppressed slave are so anti-social that no society of any kind could tolerate them. 'The very emphasis laid on the commandment "thou shalt not kill" makes it certain that we spring from an endless series of generations of murderers, who have the lust for killing in their blood, as, perhaps, we ourselves have today.'[20] And apart altogether from concern for the victims, compulsive killing satisfies no more than compulsive sex. You always want to do it again.

[19] Germaine Greer, *The Female Eunuch*, MacGibbon & Kee, 1970, p. 229 (her italics).

[20] Sigmund Freud, *Thoughts for the Times on War and Death* in *The Standard Edition of the Complete Psychological Works of Sigmund Freud*, vol. xiv, p. 285.

To indulge the body in this way, therefore, is not to restore its life, but to keep it festering in the place of the undead where it has only a tantalizing mockery of life. A further complication also follows. If the master gives his slave a half-holiday, the master will feel guilty for having allowed his slave thus to wander at large, even if the slave has broken no law of any kind known to God or man. Slaves should be in fetters, not enjoying a free afternoon. Their having a free afternoon is in itself enough to rouse their owner's guilt. (Thus, for instance, St Thomas Aquinas taught that sexual intercourse between a lawfully wedded man and wife could be without sin only if the partners at the time of intercourse were both entertaining the rational purpose of procreating children.) Apart from overt acts, what is called the rational self can feel most irrationally guilty simply by becoming aware of biological urges generally kept repressed in the subconscious, even when there has been no breach of any conceivable moral code. The body's crime is often its mere existence. It is a cause of shame unless covered with clothes. Just as slaves were not introduced to friends, so friends are not allowed to see my body.

There has of course been a strong reaction against this attempted kill-off of the body, particularly during the last two decades. Doubtless this reaction has to some small degree restored to the body its natural life. But the liberation triumphantly proclaimed and often ostentatiously paraded, has been too much in the rut of the old dualistic view of man to effect much of a genuine restoration to life. There has been a loud note of defiance in the exhibition of flesh as though its main purpose were not so much to enable people to enjoy their bodies as insolently to thumb-nose the old master – the rational faculty – and to kick him off his bloody pedestal. A man therefore remains divided. What is changing is only the balance of power between the two alienated entities of mind and body. (That is why the cult of nakedness has often gone hand in hand with the conscious and deliberate pursuit of the irrational.) The champions of body seem more concerned to prosecute the war against the oppressor within, still sneakingly felt to have considerable power, than to allow bodies simply to enjoy being bodies. When prosecuting a war, including the body's war, there is not much opportunity of having a life of your own. None the less the defiance contained in the statement 'My body is not dead, see . . . see . . .' may be a first step in restoring life. Revolt is invariably the first stage in the creation of a new order and the rebel is invariably one-sided in his attitudes. Still, there will not be much time for living so long as master and servant continue to compete with each other for domination. And that will go on until the dualistic view of man is totally abandoned.

Even in its revolt the body seems to feel its deadness. That is why the funeral parlours flourish. The embalming, painting, and dressing up of corpses is as old as civilization, modern America here having nothing to give to ancient Egypt. The object of the exercise is to give a simulacrum of life. But the vast majority of morticians in the west today have no connection with Forest Lawn or similar establishments. They are the hair stylists, clothes-designers, and manufacturers of cosmetics who have flooded the market with their skills and products. To regard the sale of their wares as in itself a sign of death would only be prejudice. Just as people drink alcohol to celebrate their happiness, so they can adorn themselves for the sheer joy of being alive. But just as people can also drink alcohol to forget their misery, so they can also use costume, paint, and perfume to disguise the corpse they feel they are. The latter motive seems the most common, since most people seem to use these commodities in an effort not to enhance but to disguise their unique individual appearance in order to look as far as possible like the stereotypes in the advertisements. Feeling that they lack life, they rush to purchase its simulacrum.

II

It is not difficult to collect evidence for the killing off of the body. It is clear enough that the flesh has been robbed of its own proper life and that the physical entity which is us has been reduced to the dimension of a slave-machine. Indeed the lifelessness of our flesh, the deadness of our body, is by far and away our chief problem and most serious danger. For these dead will not lie down. Being in hell, the place of the undead, they are always somehow planning and threatening their revenge, and they may in the end catapult us into nuclear catastrophe. The undead welcome annihilation. The body deprived of *eros* inevitably becomes the champion of *thanatos*. Better to die completely than to fester in hell. The possibility of the body's resurrection now in the present is thus of no mere theoretical interest. It is a matter of urgent concern to us all.

What does it mean?

It means my body being raised up to its own life. It means mind and body no longer making war on each other in a bid for domination, but recognizing that they are both equally me. When I can feel that I am my body, and that this does not in any way contradict the fact that I am my mind, then I shall have had experience of resurrection. For it is death which separates and life which unites. To be raised to life, therefore, is to discover that I am one person. In the experience of resurrection body and mind are no longer felt to be distinct. They function as a single entity. When I feel that my body is me, and that this is the same as my mind being me, then what I am feeling is that I am me. It is an experience which has come to most of us at some time or other. But it is generally a temporary experience which is quickly forgotten, for the bias of our basic assumptions is against it and our fear soon once again takes control. The battle for domination reasserts itself. Body and mind fall apart and compete with each other for the prize of being me. And in their falling apart the disintegration of death has set in.

Yet the experience of resurrection returns and I know myself again as one person for whom to be body is to be mind and to be mind is to be body. And this experience of oneness within myself invariably brings with it the experience of oneness with the external world. I no longer feel separated from the people and things I live among. While remaining fully themselves and preserving their own inalienable identity, they also become part of what I am. The separation between me and them is overcome so that I share an identity with them. My own resurrection is also the resurrection of the world.

But the experience of the body's resurrection cannot be set out adequately in abstract terms. What is needed is particular concrete examples. But the purpose of these examples should be made clear. They are not meant to affirm or illustrate any theological doctrine of resurrection. It will be obvious that they do not. Their purpose is simply to give flesh and blood to the attempted description of the body's resurrection now. But it may be that the examples will have points of contact with traditional Christian beliefs about the resurrection of the body in a future life, especially as these were worked out by St Paul. If so, such contacts will be illuminating, however coincidental.

12

It will be best to begin with a simple example and then to proceed later to more complex ones. The simpler the example the clearer it will be, however correspondingly limited the area of its application. So the first example will be of extremely limited application.

What is the attraction many people find in games? They are a way of taking exercise, but for their devotees they have more than this utilitarian value. We have been taught to regard them as a channel into which aggression can be harmlessly released. And doubtless it is pleasant to fight and still more pleasant to fight and win. But the opportunity a game gives me of accepting my aggressive instincts and recognizing them as myself points to something more comprehensive. Suppose that I enjoy playing tennis and am reasonably good at it. It is understood that my purpose is to beat my opponent, so there is no need for me to pretend to myself that I am not the sort of person who wants to. I am no longer a rational mind which keeps aggressive passions in a state of slavery. On the contrary, they are now welcomed as part and parcel of the me who is trying to win. But this overcoming of one form of alienation – the alienation of my aggression from what I think I am or hope I am trying to be – is symptomatic of the overcoming of all forms of alienation or division within myself. For when actually on the court playing the game I am one single undivided entity. Suppose that between sets I were to ask

myself, 'Who or what is playing tennis?' 'Well,' I should answer,
'I am.' But who or what is this I?

It is certainly me as mind, for I bring to the game all the
relevant intelligence of which I am capable. I have read a book or
two about tennis. I have occasionally been able to watch the stars
at Wimbledon and study their form. And at home I have noticed
how my friends play, the tactics they have used and the mistakes
they have made. I find that when I play, part of the attraction of
the game is the quick mental calculations it demands. It keeps you
mentally on your toes as well as physically. At the same time it
requires more than just mental intelligence. (You should see a
friend of mine, a brilliant mathematical don, trying to play. His
ineptitude is unbelievable.) Mental intelligence has to be combined with what I can only describe as sheer bodily intelligence, a
physical aptitude. It is as if the hand itself comes to know the
particular grasp of the racket needed for the particular shot. This
combination of mental and physical intelligence I find it impossible to sort out. Mental calculation is so aided and abetted by
what has become sheer physical instinct that I can't divide the
two. In the actual stroke played they are so fused and intermingled
that I can't tell where one ends and the other begins. I generally
think of them as different – that is habit I suppose – but in the
actual experience of playing they are indistinguishable. On the
court, at least when I'm on form, I don't seem to be mind and
body. I seem to be simply me. I suppose that is why the game is
satisfying. While it lasts, I am not a man divided. Everything I
am – mind and body – energizes as an organic whole, and I am
not aware of divisions and distinctions within myself. But that, as
I said, is when I am on form – which I am, as it happens, more
often than not. Tennis seems to have the power of making me
feel on form. Yet there are, naturally, days when I am not up to
scratch. My friends are very kind about it. They don't say, 'He's
not as good as he was,' but just, 'He's off-form today.'

When I'm off-form, my experience on the court is invariably
the same. It is as if I am an inner mental man who is trying to use
his body as a machine almost external to himself. It is no longer a
case of mind and body being in such perfect rapport that they are

indistinguishable. It is as if my mind begins to give orders to my body and my body resents being thus ordered about and almost deliberately fails to carry out the orders properly. My friends call it nervousness and hesitation. I am angry when my game goes to pieces like that, angry, I say, with myself. It is the anger of somebody who gives commands towards a subordinate who fails to carry them out properly. You could call it mind and body at loggerheads – of which on good days there is no trace since then the activity of mind and body is simply my activity. It's me.

When I play a game well, I have for that limited period of time an experience of the body's resurrection. For there is no hint of a dualism between mind and body with either of them trying to oppress or bully the other. I bring to the game my total undivided self, and it is that total undivided self which is active while the game is in progress. The resurrection of the body is both the resurrection of the flesh and of the entire man. The experience is illuminating even if it lasts only for an hour or two; and once the game is over I become again the efficient man of affairs who stands no nonsense from his body.

13

The second example of resurrection comes not from an athletic but an aesthetic milieu. The person to be considered is an artist – a painter. As might be expected, his experience as an artist is more complex than the experience of a tennis player.

The painter may think out some general scheme for a picture, a still-life for instance. Looking at the contents of the luncheon table, he will have some idea of the proposed picture's general outline. But before the picture actually takes shape, his mental scheme, however imaginative, will have to be complemented by the *savoir-faire* of his arm and hand. And when the picture is finished it will be different from the primary mental scheme because his intelligence of arm and hand will have left its own indispensable mark upon the canvas. Artists make preliminary sketches, cartoons and so on, of what they intend to paint. And in the course of these sketches they gradually discover what it is they intend. The full discovery is made only as the final version takes shape and the artist is standing before the canvas with palette and brush in hand. (It was G. K. Chesterton who said of a painter that his right hand taught him terrible things.) Of course, the picture, like any creative work, may not come. But when it does, the duality of mind and body is, as with the tennis player, transcended. The painter is body-mind as one single unit. And when he is painting in the fullness of his inspiration he is what we call dead to the world. He has for the time being died to everything except the picture he is in process of realizing. His identity as body-mind is totally gathered up in the performance of his creative act. His being and his work are indistinguishable. Meeting him at a party before knowing who he was he seemed just a querulous self-pitying bore. But to that identity – or lack of it – he obviously died when in his studio he was raised up as a painter of genius. And it was a resurrection of the flesh as much as anything else. Yet on an off-day, when the picture would not come, he used to grow angry with his hand because, as he put it, it would not do what he wanted it to do. Here again, as with the tennis player, the old dualism reasserted itself. The mind tried to give orders to the body as a machine and the body refused to take orders from what claimed to own it. The picture that day made no progress.

When, however, his creative potential was being successfully articulated and the picture progressing rapidly, it was not only the duality of mind and body which was overcome but also that between the objects painted and the artist's vision of them. In the limited area of the luncheon table (the picture's theme) the external world had ceased to be merely external and had also become part and parcel of the painter's own being. Which, he used sometimes to ask himself, was more real – the things on the table or the vision of them which was appearing on the canvas? He never knew the answer because in the circumstances the question was irrelevant and had no meaning. For the things on the table had ceased to be simply things on the table and had also become the self to which his painting was giving expression. Yet the picture was by no means the self-indulgence of a private fantasy or the mere projection of his own ego on to the canvas, which told you nothing except about himself. His loyalty to what he saw was strict and absolute and it showed you something which was there but which you had been unable to see before. It was rather that what he saw had ceased to be divided from himself. The distance between painter and what was painted had been obliterated. The two had become one. It was as if his own resurrection had been accompanied by a transformation of the external world in which its real identity had become inseparable from his own. He had somehow smashed into and broken up the hard externality of the things on the luncheon table and had raised them to a newness of life in which their separability from himself had been overcome. And the completed picture handed on the same experience, though to a lesser degree, to its viewers. Looking at the picture they felt less separated than usual from the external world, and they sensed the absurd but glorious possibility of being in communion with knives and forks and a table-cloth. Here we have a glimpse of the resurrection not only of the flesh but of the world, of which St Paul was able to give us no more than a tantalizing hint when he spoke of the whole creation obtaining, like ourselves, the glorious liberty of the children of God.[21] In the light of the artist's experience and our own as we view his picture, St Paul's words begin to have meaning not as a scientific or philosophical theory but as a fact which has been lived. These things are, even if we know not how they can be.

14

Looking round for examples of the resurrection of the body, the flesh, we are bound, sooner or later, to find ourselves in the company of lovers. Their presence here is inevitable, and we had better learn from them what we can.

We shall have, though, to tread with some delicacy, the delicacy not of the timid but of the shrewd. For it is a commonplace that love is liable to neurotic distortion, and we must not confuse the compulsions of the slave undead with the freedom of the

[21] Romans 8:21.

resurrected flesh. (This confusion, incidentally, has bedevilled the discussion of sexual ethics. Those, for instance, who admire the insight of D. H. Lawrence often fail to make clear that his theme is the resurrection of the flesh and not the berserk behaviour of the slave let loose for the afternoon.) At the same time we must not be too finicky. For in experience compulsion and resurrection are often mixed up together. Indeed the experience of resurrection often grows from what was originally an experience of compulsion. If we are perfectionists or purists here we shall find ourselves cut off from all experience of love. What is true of religious devotion is also true of human love – illusion is often the midwife of reality and if we are paralysed by the fear of illusion the reality will remain permanently undiscovered.

The hero of our story is George. And the story will be told from his point of view. It could, of course, also be told from the point of view of Margaret, the woman he eventually married. But the attempt to tell it from both points of view at once would be unnecessarily confusing.

George had a rather strict upbringing. This in itself might have done him nothing but good, except that the strictness contained a marked element of fear, especially fear of the physical. Defecating and urinating were regarded as unpleasant necessities and not as subjects for family comment, let alone humour. George said later that he never saw his father fondle or hug anything except the dog. His parents weren't mean, but they had a horror of what they called over-indulgence. George remembered that his mother once bought some strawberries for lunch – he must have been thirteen or fourteen at the time – and he was rebuked for greeting them over-enthusiastically. 'Gosh, I *love* strawberries,' he'd said, and his mother had answered a little chillingly – 'You can't *love* food, George. You can like strawberries, not love them,' and she kept an unusually large amount for the charwoman in the kitchen so that there would be no second helpings.

The discovery of sexual impulses in adolescence came to George as a relief. From his first going to school at six or seven he had always felt that other boys were more alive than he was, though as a child he wouldn't have been able to put it like that nor to identify the situation for what it was – that his body had consistently been put to death while the other boys' bodies were alive. Anyhow, the arrival of adolescence enabled George to find life for his body. He masturbated and went with other boys and later with girls. By such behaviour he was able to show himself that he was as much alive as any of his friends. After all, he did what they did and probably more often. He found what he'd been taught to call sensual indulgence not merely pleasurable (like everybody else) but a kind of death-defying sacrament. It became for him an assertion of his physical identity against the denial of it by his parents. It was the most felt way he could be himself.

He would have been scared if his parents had known about what he did, and he was careful to see that they didn't. If for some reason or other he was feeling low, sickening for flu or nervous about an approaching exam, then he would feel guilty about his behaviour. Perhaps it would be more accurate to say that his guilt then rose explicitly to the surface. Otherwise, when things were normal, his guilt about being a body was more like an atmosphere he was vaguely aware of and which he decided to ignore. It was difficult to say really whether his sexual activity was more an assertion of identity or a defiance of this background of guilt. But no doubt these were two sides of the same coin.

By the time he was eighteen and went to university, he was ready for a showdown with his parents. He was no longer going to pretend that his body was dead, like his parents wanted. They talked as if his first sexual experience would be in about ten years' time when he married a 'nice' girl – 'nice' meant dehydrated, the sort of girl no man anywhere, even when drunk, would ever dream of calling a peach. So, during the vacs, George began bringing home the girls he was having affairs with. The more sensual their looks and lascivious their gestures, the better was the point made. But the chill in the atmosphere at home was too much even for the combined crusading ardour of George and girl. He soon began spending his vacs elsewhere. And after he got a degree and found a job, he hardly ever went home at all.

His affairs never lasted very long. The record was fourteen months, the average, four or five. After he had run through half a dozen girls, he slowly realized that he didn't feel much more alive than he had done as a young boy at home. Sex had played a curious trick on him. At first it had promised to be life-giving. It had given him the sensation of coming into his body as a prince comes into his kingdom. But now it seemed to be paying off less and less adequately. The business of intercourse and orgasm had somehow lost a great deal of its magic. It had become too much of a mechanical operation, like shooting targets at a fair. He found that he was himself less and less involved in what he did. The contemporary girl seemed little more than a servicing machine, and what she serviced – George's body – was itself little more than a machine.

A moralist might have given himself the satisfaction of regarding this state of affairs as the reward of vice. But it would have been a superficial diagnosis. What was fundamental here was not vice or virtue in any conventional sense, but the deadness of George's body and his inability to raise it from the dead. That deadness was the result of his early conditioning (in that sense at least he had been conceived and born in sin). By both precept and example George had been taught to regard his body not as an essential part of himself but as something he should master, subdue, and order about. The subduing and ordering about was to be done by him as mind. And it was this separation of his body from his mind which George was not able to remedy. When he began having girls and living with them, it felt at first as though he had delivered himself from slavery to his mind so that his body could come into its own. But the body which he thus indulged was still alienated from him. It was still no more than a machine. Its initial promise of bringing him life and identity had come to nothing because even in its pleasures George could not help keeping his body at arm's length from himself. His fundamental separation from the girls he lived with was the inevitable result of this prior and primal separation of his body from his mind. It was thus that George found himself in the city of the undead. His body had no life. Its functioning, even in matters of pleasure, was mechanical. It looked as if it had been killed off for good and all. Of course he could deny his body its mechanical pleasure. That, he thought, is what the parsons would have told him to do. But living what they called a chaste life would not have raised him from the dead. For him in his situation it would have been no more than a final capitulation to his body's deadness, an unconditional surrender to death in the midst of life. It was one thing being dead. It was another thing to agree to being dead. Thus to agree would have been like taking a pride in the fact (as his parents seemed to), and George was incapable of that final hypocrisy.

So he continued to sleep around.

One of the women he slept with was a typist at his office called Margaret. He was more than usually attracted to her physically. But when they began living together he had no idea that this would turn out to be more than just another of his casual affairs. Yet after two or three months he noticed that his feelings for her had begun to be different from what he had felt about the other girls. He enjoyed sex with her, but the sex had begun to be more than a dead-end. With the other girls, when he woke up in the morning he invariably felt – 'Oh God, she's here.' But with Margaret he had begun to wake up feeling that there was something especially good about life at the moment and had immediately realized it was Margaret's presence. She seemed to see what lay behind the ferocity of his passion, that there was a dead man trying to come alive. And it became clear that she loved him, deadness and all. She wasn't taken in by George the lecher. Nor was she put off by the man the lecher was trying to escape. She saw everything George was and loved it, and her love enabled George to value himself, including his bodily passion. She made him feel his physical feelings were lovable – part and parcel of the man she loved. George wasn't explicitly aware that his attitude to himself was changing, but he became very much aware of how deeply he was beginning to value Margaret. The more secure he felt in her love, the less violent his passion became. Its keynote had ceased to be ferocity and had become serenity. Sex was no longer a way of proving anything. It was a way of being. Clearly they were deeply in love.

After living together for about a year, they decided to get

married. George had never thought that he would actually want to get married, let alone that he would look forward to the prospect with such enthusiasm. It showed conclusively, he thought, how different were his feelings for Margaret from those he had had for other girls.

What surprised him now was not so much the strength of his sexual feelings (he had been used to that) as their depth. Previously he had had no idea that he could feel about a woman so totally as he felt about Margaret. His body had ceased to be anything even remotely resembling a machine. It was him. It gathered up everything he was into the one glory of his love for Margaret. There was not the slightest hint of a division between body and mind. George knew with a comprehensive certainty that Margaret was the girl for him. He said Yes to her at every level of his being. How amusingly and endearingly shrewd she was in her comments about other people. How sensible she was in practical matters. And if her opinion of a play or a book (she hadn't been to university) was not what a professional critic would say, it generally had a great deal of point to it, even if at first it seemed attractively uninformed and funny. George used to laugh and say to her, even in public, 'You're the stupidest woman I've ever met.' She never minded as she knew he meant the opposite, and they enjoyed the embarrassment it sometimes caused their less perceptive friends. George admitted to himself that he had met more academically intelligent girls than Margaret (Yes, Christ he had), prettier girls, more obviously attractive girls, girls who were more sexually clued up or more socially competent. But they didn't begin to be Margaret. It was odd to think how lifeless he had felt before he'd met her, how deadly his existence. Now he felt alive as never before, so alive that the past was just non-life. Of course to live now was not simply to be George, but to be George with Margaret as an essential part of him. His identity had expanded to include hers. And far from this meaning that he was closed up against the rest of the world (the part that wasn't Margaret), the very opposite was the case. The stars in the sky now seemed to belong to him – he'd hardly noticed them before. He splashed about in the rain like a small child enjoying his bath. He seemed to be in closer touch with everybody he met and they in their turn seemed more friendly. Even his parents seemed lovable even if slightly pathetic – he wanted to love them into life. Aunt Agatha's jokes seemed funny. He was in communion with everybody and everything. All things were his. He was reminded of a phrase he had read in *The Rainbow*: 'Self was a oneness with the infinite. To be oneself was a supreme gleaming triumph of infinity.' Formerly those words of Lawrence had seemed utter nonsense, high falutin' and meaningless. Now they described exactly how he felt.

A year or two later the initial excitement cooled down, the excitement of novelty. George grew more accustomed to being loved and to loving. But there had been no mistake. Margaret continued to be the woman for him. If there had been a degree of illusion, if, for instance, Margaret's judgement of people was not so unerring as it once seemed, or if superficially she was not quite the angel of unselfishness she had formerly appeared, it was the kind of illusion which prepared you for the reality. It was a revealing not a deceptive illusion – rather like Father Christmas, the discovery of whose non-existence does nothing to spoil the children's delight in the festivities of the season. After he had fallen in love with Margaret George had used a lot of gold, too much, in his initial portrait of her. But there are other no less attractive colours, even if less immediately obvious. And as some of the gold wore off these other colours were revealed.

Here in George's story we see, if anywhere, the resurrection of the flesh. The dead body of what was a mere machine was raised up to a new life of glory. When in the words of the marriage service George said to Margaret, 'With my body I thee worship,' it was a statement of literal fact. George did not worship Margaret in his mind and therefore constrain his body to go through the physical postures of worship. It was with its own inherent life that George's body worshipped Margaret and thereby found its own inherent joy and fulfilment. But the body could not do this in terms of the old dualistic assumption about man. In the resurrection of George's flesh the dualism between mind and matter, soul and body, ego and id, was, as in our previous examples, overcome. George when he stood with Margaret at the altar was an undifferentiated unity of body-mind. And it was an inclusive not an exclusive wholeness. Margaret for George had ceased to be simply an external object. The distance between them had been obliterated. That is not to say that Margaret had ceased for George to live in her own right. She did not lose her in-alienable identity as Margaret (just as for the painter the things on the luncheon table continued to be themselves, and he observed towards them in his picture a strict and absolute loyalty). But now Margaret's inalienable identity no longer separated her from George but united her to him. And the same was true, if in a lesser degree, of the world he lived in. Even the sun and moon were no longer strangers.

This experience of union is an integral part of resurrection. The transcendence of the mind-body antimony brings with it, in the particular space one is inhabiting, the abolition of externality as no more than sheer externality. Or to put it in simpler terms, if all the world loves a lover, that is because a lover first loves all the world.

15

Seven or eight years after George and Margaret married, George's father died. He had managed his financial affairs carefully so that George's mother – her name was Emily – was left comfortably provided for. She was now in her early sixties. She sensibly refused to make her home with her son and daughter-in-law. She sold the old house and bought a smaller one. She had decided that once she was properly installed in the new house she would do nothing, at least for the time being, except to have a few friends to tea occasionally and perhaps to lend a hand at the church fête. She enjoyed reading and there was always the television.

Emily hadn't quite realized the extent to which she would miss her husband. Their relationship had never been warm, and it had soon settled down to what only their self-control kept from being intolerably boring. But running the house and looking after her husband had given Emily something to do. Her being occupied had protected her from realizing how isolated she was. Not that she hadn't a number of friends, some of them extremely good friends. Her isolation was on a more fundamental level. She was isolated from a great deal of what a woman is – there were whole areas of tenderness and sympathy and compassion and intuitive understanding from which she was permanently excluded. Her approach to life had been too cerebral. She was too much a stranger to deep feeling. George saw this when he compared her with Margaret. What, he thought, his mother had always refused to be was a body. She'd been able to ignore this when she'd had his father to look after, but now she was beginning to realize how empty her life was. Every time George saw her she looked more withdrawn. She had ceased now laying down the law in that neat emphatic way which gave you the impression that she had worked everything out logically and knew it all. But her no longer wishing to impose her views left her without a role. And that made her seem that she wasn't there, both to herself and others. Her conversation with George and Margaret was forced and formal – about things acquaintances might have discussed at a sherry party. She didn't inhabit what she said. It was just talking to keep up appearances. Her husband's death, confronting her inescapably not so much with what she was but with what she wasn't, made her feel that she was dead too. And she showed it. George thought she probably wouldn't live much longer, although she was only sixty-four.

But George was wrong. Emily was reckoned a sensible woman, and she was soon roped in by the local branch of the Samaritans. At first her inclination was to refuse. She wasn't at all impressed when the organizer, an old acquaintance, said solemnly to her, 'We need you, Emily.' She saw through that sort of appeal. But she was driven to accept by the impact of her own emptiness. If she was to forget it, she must find something to take her mind off it, what looking after her husband and running the house had previously done for her. So she joined the Samaritans. This slowly involved her in all kinds of contacts. Her duties as a Samaritan were of course clearly defined and limited. But gradually she allowed them to lead on to other things. She kept track of the people who sought her help and this led her to meeting their families and friends, and then the friends of friends. If she hadn't already abandoned her neat limited logic, she would have had to now. It wouldn't have been the slightest use to the people she got to know. It wouldn't have given them a hope in hell. What she didn't realize at first was that she was beginning to grow quite fond of them.

In the unsatisfactoriness of their lives, their obvious need, their muddled hopelessness, she began in fact to find a bond with them, because what they so obviously and openly were, she herself was too, not on the surface but deep inside. She was stuck with nothing she could really call herself. Yet her being able to sympathize, her sense of kinship with the obviously stricken, showed that something after all was there which was beginning to come alive. She didn't realize how much it had grown until one afternoon she was with a fat working woman whose husband had recently left her. Emily remembered how badly the woman smelt. She had doubtless been too distraught to wash. Words were obviously useless. The woman was well beyond being comforted by anything that could be said. Emily found herself going up to her and taking her in her arms and hugging her. It was an involuntary gesture, a spontaneous going out to need in the most natural way, the only possible way. Emily cried a little herself. It was partly deep fellow-feeling for the deserted wife. But it was also partly joy at the discovery of physical warmth. The woman in yielding to Emily's hugs and finding comfort in them had given Emily some kind of fundamental assurance about herself – that she was and could be physical in the most natural and unforced sort of way. The incident signalled her discovery and acceptance of her body. As she walked home from the woman's house Emily was convulsed with tears. The woman was coming to supper, but it was not for her that Emily was crying now. Her tears were simply tears of joy. Something always missing from her life had been found. And what ran through her mind and made her cry all the more were words she had known from childhood but which had never struck her before – 'Bring forth the best robe, and put it on him; and put a ring on his hand and shoes on his feet; and bring hither the fatted calf, and kill it; and let us eat and be merry: for this my son was dead and is alive again; he was lost and is found.'

She often took people's arms after that, and sometimes kissed and hugged them. It wasn't anything artificial. It certainly wasn't gush, still less was it a calculated therapeutic policy. It was because that kind of physical contact expressed what she felt at the time. She loved these people. And her love gave her understanding. She intuitively recognized that at the root of much of their trouble, as of her own, there lay their rejected and unloved bodies. Yet she couldn't have expounded this in a talk or paper. She hardly knew she knew.

The following Christmas she went to a party and enjoyed it too much to be aware that she was enjoying it. Some friends gave her a lift home. She unlocked her front door, turned the lights on, took off her coat and shoes, and sat down in the kitchen. 'Heavens above,' she said out loud to herself, 'I'm rather drunk.' She was too amused to keep the joke to herself. Next morning she telephoned two or three friends to laugh over it with them.

16

An attempt has been made to show how in the case of a tennis player, a painter, a lover, and a widow, their bodies were raised from the dead. Has this experience of resurrection now in the present any points of contact with traditional Christian beliefs about the resurrection of the body in a future life?

Certainly in the experience of the four people described there are obvious similarities to St Paul's teaching about the future resurrection-body.

There is first of all the paradox of continuity combined with discontinuity, of identity combined with difference. This was of course worked out in varying degrees in the various examples, and was more pronounced in some than others. But it was present in all four. In the tennis player it was present only to a limited degree for a very limited time. During the hour or two of his game some of his bodily instincts were received and accepted as himself. But for all this limitation there was none the less a difference between the man on the court and the busy executive in his office. At tennis he was a different person although also the same one. This was true in a fuller degree of the painter. The egocentric self-pitying bore he tended to be on social occasions was completely transformed when in his studio he was painting in the fullness of his inspiration. But he was also the same man. So too George was still George after his love for Margaret had made a new man of him. And Emily was still Emily after she had discovered and accepted her body. Yet the change in these two was fundamental. They were in the deepest sense different people, although also the same.

Secondly, the resurrection of the body, both in the future as described by St Paul and as experienced now in the present, brought access to hitherto inaccessible sources of vitality. The body in its low estate as a dead object to be pushed around was raised up to a life of glory, even if the glory was of varying degrees. For what such triumphs are worth, the body won a tennis match. The painter's body produced a work of genius. George's body in his love for Margaret was experienced as a oneness with the infinite, while Emily's brought her to a rich peace she had never previously known.

Thirdly, the overcoming of the body-mind dualism spread out to overcome the separating distance between self and the world. The tennis player on form felt on top of the world. The painter discovered what he painted as bone of his bone and flesh of his flesh. George felt at one with the stars and the rain, not to mention the people he met. Emily saw herself in others and was thus able to love her neighbour as herself because she came to love herself as she did her neighbour. Whatever else St Paul intended to convey by his image of the spiritual body, it certainly included this transcendence of separability. If the whole creation was to share the glorious liberty of the children of God, what else was this but the recognition of our identity with it?

It is not in any way being claimed that the true meaning of St Paul's words have at length been unearthed. That would be the kind of foolishness possible only to those with no sense of humour.

What, however, is being pointed out is that there are parallels between St Paul's description of the future and our own experience of the present. Since it is only the present which is with us and the future in the nature of the case can only be theoretical (however firm the grounds for our theory), perhaps we should be more concerned with the resurrection of the body now than with its resurrection in some unknown future beyond the grave. For not to be concerned with the present is the hallmark of evasion. Neither orthodoxy nor spirituality can afford the expedient of making *mañana* its password. 'Behold now is the accepted time. Behold now is the day of salvation.'[22]

17

But how, then, can we make this experience of resurrection our own?

One thing is certain. A man cannot lift himself by his own bootstring. A dead body cannot raise itself from the dead. Invariably what we would like is a formula, a technique, a programme, something, as we say, that we can get our teeth into. But if a formula is what we want, what we need is a miracle. For nothing less than a miracle can give life to the dead. But miracles are chancy because they are beyond our own control to effect. So the temptation is strong to cease looking for miracles and to do as energetically as possible what we can do. This would be sensible enough except that it keeps our eyes averted from the arrival of new possibilities. For it is the man who tries hard to get himself newness of life who succeeds only in shutting himself up against it. That is inevitable, since the self who tries is the self organized by means of the very dualistic status quo which has to be challenged and changed. And the status quo is confirmed by the effort, not weakened or overthrown. That is the trap into which all ascetics and perfectionists fall. In their attempts to overcome the alienation of their bodies from the rest of what they are, that alienation can only be more firmly established, since the weapon

[22] 2 Corinthians 6:2.

they employ is the very dualism of mind and body from which the alienation springs.

It was only when the Buddha gave up the austerities he had been practising – and the five ascetics living with him had departed in disgust – that enlightenment came to him. It was only when St Paul gave up trying to keep the law and instead saw and received what was offered to him that he found salvation. And he described this salvation as a new creation, the raising up of a new being, not as the overhaul and repair of the old one by frantic effort. 'Asked why he meditated all day long, a pupil replied that he desired to become a Buddha. The Master picked up a brick and began to rub it. Asked what he was doing, he explained that he wished to make a mirror. "But no amount of polishing a brick will make a mirror." "If so, no amount of sitting cross-legged will make thee a Buddha," was the deep reply.'[23] So in Zen, which is taught through the practice of archery, one of the lessons most emphasized is that one should be able to hit the target without aiming.

The point is really simple enough. If the body is dead because it has been cut off from the rest of what we are, then it cannot be raised from the dead like an inanimate object which is lifted up or pushed around. What it needs is to have its own life given to it so that it can raise itself by its own inherent vitality. And this can happen only when the dualism between mind and body has been transcended. It is something we can neither think nor act ourselves into. There is no escaping the necessity of miracle.

But the essence of miracle is not that it is dramatic, nor that it interferes with the natural world regarded as an external structure which works according to its own laws. Miracle is not what we invoke when science appears to have failed. The essence of miracle is our discovery of what we are. The discovery is miraculous because the previous organization of our being provided no vantage point from which we could have seen what now we do see. Our new vision has come to us. It has arrived from we know not where. It has not been put together from insights already possessed, however well those insights fall into place once the

[23] Christmas Humphreys, *Buddhism*, Penguin Books, 1951, p. 184.

new vision has come and possessed us. There can therefore be no
evidence for miracle, if by evidence we mean the public exhibition of some change in the world observed as external reality. For
the change comes to the observer not to what is observed. It is not
a case of saying – 'Look at that now.' The testimony to miracle
can only be – 'Whereas once I was blind, now I can see.' If, for
instance, George's love for Margaret raised his body from the
dead, that was because he saw Margaret as no other man did. The
change had occurred to George in the discovery that he could
love totally with every fibre of his being. Margaret was instrumental in that discovery, but she did not cause it. To make his
point it would be useless for George to exhibit Margaret. He
could only appeal to similar experiences his friends have had with
regard to the women they love. Or when the painter discovered
his vision while painting his picture and revealed the things on the
luncheon table as somehow caught up in our own identity, it
would have been absurd for him to have brought people up to his
studio to see the knives and forks for themselves. The miracle
was the painter's ability to see. And if his picture enabled its
viewers to see things in some degree as he saw them, that is
because the miracle of one man's vision can effect a similar
miracle in the vision of others. The picture did not prove anything in any objective or scientific sense. It was not a public
demonstration of the kind produced by scientists. Emily did not
try to get life. She found it unexpectedly. The tennis player was
interested in the game for its own sake. The release he found in
it was incidental.

18

If, therefore, the resurrection of the body requires a miracle, it is
a miracle of discovery – the miracle by which I find that I am
both more and other than I had previously imagined. And this
discovery of myself is invariably accompanied by the kindred
discovery that I belong intimately to the world in which I live
and which I now feel belongs to me. For the distance between me
and my world has been eliminated, so that my own identity
includes what I see and what I see includes my own identity.

The occasion for this miracle is the common day-to-day experience of ordinary men and women – the existence of tennis as a game; the accident of George's having met Margaret and Margaret's responsiveness; the tradition of painting in our culture and the availability of canvas and pigments; the fact that the Samaritan organization existed in Emily's town. These were the occasions of self-discovery, the sacramental means by which the discovery was mediated. But they were not its cause. For tennis, Margaret, painting and the Samaritans leave most people cold enough to continue living as exactly the same individuals as before. The actual cause of the self-discovery was the mysterious creativity of life itself, the fact that life possesses the potency to create what is new, so that we are changed and find ourselves alive as we weren't before. It is thus that through the sacramental medium of common circumstance we hear the voice of the Eternal Word, and hearing are created. For the Eternal Word is not a cult-object in the possession of the churches nor an esoteric device traded by the mystagogues. It is the creative voice that speaks by means of anything or everything which impinges upon us in the ordinary business of our daily lives.

It is obvious that the dualism between mind and body cannot be overcome on the level on which that dualism is established. What we need is to be raised from that level. And this raising of us up can be effected only by what comes to us from beyond our present view of ourselves and shakes it out of recognition, however ordinary may be the occasion of the coming. Yet what thus comes to us from beyond what we know of ourselves is not felt as an alien intruder taking command. For its power is experienced precisely as the power to be what we most truly and fully are, like the characters in our stories. Creation does not impose upon what it creates. Creation makes it what it is.

It follows that to be created is to be affirmed. Such affirmation of what we are is a major element in our experience of resurrection. We could say that if our bodies are raised from the dead that is because they are felt to be accepted and affirmed. It is only in virtue of that acceptance and affirmation of our physical being that we can rise above the division of ourselves into mind and body – that is into master and slave. The master cannot free the slave as he feels most guiltily uncomfortable for doing so. The slave cannot free himself from his master. All he can do is to revolt, and in all revolt the power of the master is acknowledged. But the word of acceptance and affirmation passes beyond the range of this division and the impasse it imposes, for it comes from beyond the self we have known; and it is addressed to us in our undivided totality so that the whole of what we are is called forth into newness of life. Because it is the creative Word, it establishes our identity and makes us feel more fully ourselves than before.

If the dualistic view of man is, as we have seen, his attempt to grapple with the experience of fear, it is by the word of acceptance and affirmation that the fear is exorcized. Perfect love casts out fear, as the New Testament says – the perfect creative love which is the source and ground of all we are and which is mediated to us by means of the common circumstances of our daily lives.

In what is to us the strange idiom and terminology of first-century Jewish legalism, it was of this creative Word of acceptance that St Paul spoke in his teaching about justification by faith. Man is no longer a slave in bondage to fear. He knows himself accepted as a son of God and the infinite freedom which that brings with it.

However they might attempt to describe it, it was the same experience which came to the characters we have described. They too, like St Paul, heard the voice of the Eternal Word. St Paul as a pharisee heard the Word through the medium of the religious interests which were his chief concern. The characters in our stories heard the Word through the medium of their respective preoccupations. But whatever the medium, fear was cast out. Dualism was transcended. And those concerned were raised in their bodies to newness of life. St Paul at times reverted to the fear and the dualism. So doubtless did our characters, if their story could be told in full.

19

But there still remains an unanswered and unanswerable question. It is the sore fact of human inequality of which social and economic inequality is but the tip of the iceberg. Of two people the one is taken and the other is left. Some are given life while others appear to be allowed to fester. There is a brutality here vividly described by St Paul in his picture of the Lord loving Jacob but hating Esau for no reason whatever since it was before either of them was born.[24]

If the resurrection of the body cannot be contrived, if it requires a miracle, then what are we to do about it? If I cannot raise myself by my own bootstrings, then what action is left to me? If the brick will not become a mirror by being rubbed, what other possibility remains except that of total passivity?

In this connection there is a paradox noted by all the great teachers of mankind. The good shepherd, said Jesus, goes out and finds the lost sheep. But the Prodigal Son takes the initiative and himself returns to his father's house. St Paul taught that God, because he is creator, calls the non-existent into existence. It was thus that God called us to salvation. Yet, says St Paul, 'Work out your own salvation with fear and trembling.'[25] For the Buddha enlightenment meant the end of all striving, for striving was the result of the illusory fancies of itself and its world entertained by the closed-up ego. Yet the Buddha's last words to his disciples were, 'Work out your salvation with diligence.'

Useful here are some words Jesus addressed to the religious élite of his day – 'You know how to interpret the appearance of the sky [to forecast the weather], but you cannot interpret the signs of the times.'[26] When our fear keeps us imprisoned in the dualistic assumption about ourselves, it is easy for us to direct all our efforts to the maintenance of that status quo, and hence not to understand what is happening to us when the status quo is threatened. The threat comes always from our own feelings, but those feelings are aroused by what we see and hear. A television programme, for instance, may arouse strong feelings which constitute a threat to the dualistic status quo because they remind us forcibly of the body and its claims to freedom and life. But we fail to interpret this sign of the times. As far as possible we ignore the feelings aroused, or rather we divert them against themselves

[24] Romans 9:13.   [25] Philippians 2:12.   [26] Matthew 16:3.

so that we become indignant about the programme we've seen and condemn it in the name of public morality and decency. What should have been a sign which hinted to us that our view of ourselves was narrow and stifling is construed as a call to redouble our efforts at suffocation. If, however, we are to work out our salvation with diligence, we must be prepared to accept the confusion and turmoil of our feelings and not to deny or condemn any of them out of hand. For the threat they contain may be only to the limited view of ourselves which must be destroyed in order that a more adequate view may take its place. If we cannot raise ourselves from the dead, we can, to some extent at least, unplug our ears to hear the voice of the Eternal Word in things which threaten to turn us upside down and inside out. It may be a television programme. It may be the behaviour of the young. It may be somebody with whom we have fallen in love. It may be some predicament we are in. It may be the strength of our unsatisfied desires. It may be success or failure. It may be a public event which monopolizes the headlines. It may be anything. For in everything we must be open to receive the Eternal Word whose call is both the destruction and resurrection of what we are. It is above all by the open mind and the open heart, the willingness to abandon even what seem the most sacred of our prejudices, the willingness to think and feel what we are out afresh, it is by that openness, and that alone, that we can work out our salvation. And certainly it will be with fear and trembling. For the unknown threatens before it gives life. The beast roars before we discover that he is Prince Charming himself. This openness requires discipline and courage of a heroic kind, and neither religious devotion nor moral earnestness is any guarantee of its presence. 'Watch, therefore, for you know neither the day nor the hour.'[27] It is only by being on the alert for change within ourselves that we shall interpret the sign of the times, and so be ready to hear the voice of the Eternal Word.

There is hope here as well as demand. For since the Eternal Word can speak through any and every circumstance, we can never conclude that our own or other people's outward or inner

[27] Matthew 25:13.

circumstances are altogether too unfavourable for the miracle of resurrection to occur. Charity to ourselves and others requires that we ameliorate those circumstances as much as possible. But when all is said and done it remains true that it is neither promising people nor lucky people nor deserving people nor likely people who are raised from the dead, but precisely dead people. The background of resurrection is always impossibility. And with impossibility staring us in the face, the prelude to resurrection is invariably doubt, confusion, strife, and the cynical smile which is our defence against them. Resurrection is always the defiance of the absurd.

Our physical, emotional, and sexual disabilities, therefore, do not exclude us from the resurrection of the body. They can be the very means whereby the creativity of life takes hold of us. And as it does, we shall find ourselves accepting what we are and no longer wishing we were something else (the content of our waking fantasies). Unless we are literally in the last stages of physical illness we shall discover that what we are can bring its own bodily fulfilment. Only we must not be hypnotized by the stereotypes and their brash assumption that fulfilment can come only within the narrow limits of the images they purvey, or we shall be like a man dying of thirst by a mountain stream because there is no tap for him to turn on. *Eros*, with its roots deep in sexual feeling, can by acceptance be diffused throughout our entire physical structure so that every contact we have with others and the world we live in can be an act of physical love. It requires a miracle. But it is a miracle which has occurred to many men and women, and from which our disabilities in no way exclude us.

If to openness of mind and heart we add a measure of expectancy, then we shall be looking for the resurrection of the body which is the resurrection of the flesh. And if we are thus seeking, must it not mean that we have begun to find?

CHAPTER THREE

RESURRECTION & MIND

THE resurrection of the body consists in the discovery that it is myself and not a machine I own. Like the body, the mind too is in need of resurrection. For, although considered the master who is or ought to be in charge of what I am, the mind is often, none the less, like the body, considered as no more than a machine; not, it is true, a slave-machine in a condition of subservience, but a machine which controls because it can observe and calculate. When I equate myself with what I call mind, I am generally equating myself with an instrument which by its calculations gains intellectual mastery of what it observes.

The mastery has produced rich results. Civilization itself depends upon man's ability to control his environment. Yet when I equate myself with my mind and my mind with no more than this observing, calculating, and controlling machine, then the intellectual mastery achieved is in the last resort self-defeating.

For if I consider myself no more than a thinking machine and reduce my personal identity to the equivalent of a computer, then I am out of touch with a great deal of what I am. Half of me is alienated from the other half. And this falling apart is a sign of death, as disintegration always is. The alienated mind-machine, while promising to enrich me, in fact bleeds me of life. It becomes a death-dealing tyrant.

An extreme instance of this state of affairs can be found in the achievements of nuclear physics. Here the mind as a calculating and controlling machine has achieved one of its greatest triumphs – and has thereby reduced mankind to the condition of a prisoner awaiting execution. For nuclear physics means the nuclear bomb.

What, however, we have most to fear from the mind-machine is probably not sudden annihilation in a nuclear catastrophe, but the gradual draining away of our life which follows from the reduction of reality to the dehydrated mental constructs which are supposed to convey it. It is easy enough for us to confuse these symbols of reality with the reality itself, to make thinking into a substitute for living. If I peruse a map in the stuffiness of my study, is not this the same thing as walking in the open country which the map charts? So a large part of what I am is uncared and uncatered for. In consequence it begins to atrophy, leaving me with a sense of final frustration.

What is needed here is a resurrection of the mind whereby it is raised well above its calculating and controlling functions and is discovered to be, like the body, the living feeling person I am, the person made for involvement and communion with my world. Only then will the mind bring me the full richness which belongs to my human nature.

2

In talking about the mind I realize that I am here wandering on to land which has been very highly cultivated for over 2,000 years. Since men began to think systematically, one of their major concerns has been to define accurately the nature of mind and its place in the general order of things. One of the main tasks of philosophy has been to investigate the relation which may be said to exist between the person who thinks and the content of his thought. And since what we think about is the external world, it is the relation between the thinking self and what we apprehend as external objects which has been the stock-in-trade of philosophical investigation. Some philosophers have regarded the mind as no more than a mirror in which the external world is reflected. Others have regarded the external world as the creation of the mind – something which apart from the mind has no independent reality of its own. Others again have regarded the mind as organizing what it perceives into its own inherent categories or patterns, so that the content of the mind is not the external world as it is in itself, but that world cut up and arranged into the predetermined mental moulds.

The ambiguity which surrounds the relation between the mind and the objects it perceives is reflected in the parallel ambiguities surrounding the use of the word reason. Reason can mean the ability to put two and two together and so to arrive at a conclusion by logical inference. It can mean what in common parlance is called intuition, where there is no logical process of reasoning in the above sense but a direct and immediate hunch concerning something – what could be called insight or shrewdness. Or reason can mean the ability to recognize and appreciate a quality like beauty which resides in things and is revealed by them.

Meanwhile Freud's discoveries have added their own complications. Freud, we could say, had good reason for believing that men often use their reason to give a varnish of rational plausibility to conclusions already reached by other kinds of processes – the compulsive desires and fears of the subconscious mind. Hence his dismissal of philosophy as 'a decorative centre-piece',[1] even though his own conclusions were founded upon the firm if unrecognized metaphysical assumptions of nineteenth-century materialism.

3

My concern here, however, is not philosophical in the strict professional sense. I shall not discuss the respective merits and defects of the various theories of knowledge. Just as in the last chapter I considered the general unexamined background of assumption on the basis of which people in practice thought of and treated their bodies, so here I shall consider the same general unexamined background of assumption held by people with regard to their minds and the uses to which in practice their minds can be put. The same dualism of mind and body is of course in evidence. But now it will be considered from the side of mind.

What happens when the mind is separated from the rest of what I am?

Most obviously there comes a comforting clarity in the mind's understanding of itself. The mind in isolation seems no more than a machine which observes and calculates. By thus observing the external world and putting two and two together about it the mind is able in some measure to control it. And this control is

[1] Ernest Jones, *Sigmund Freud: Life and Work*, vol. 2, Hogarth Press, 1955, p. 96.

exercised without the thinking self becoming personally involved in what is controlled. Indeed, the observing self, if it is to be free from prejudice and to see what is before it as clearly as possible, must remain strictly detached from what it observes. This detachment is called objectivity. And it has been by the disciplined exercise of this detachment, by strict adherence to the demands of objectivity, that scientists have been able to achieve their results. In establishing a conclusion the scientist first observes his material and sees how it works. On the basis of this observation he makes the appropriate calculations. And the end result is his intellectual mastery of what he has observed. It becomes his mental possession even if he is not concerned to control it physically or such control (as with astronomy) is out of the question. And in the process the vagaries of his own feelings and temperament, all that he is except his mind as an observing and calculating machine, have been rigorously excluded.

The achievements of science either in terms of pure knowledge or of its ability to ameliorate our human condition are too obvious to need discussing. It is enough to think of what has been discovered by the radio telescope or the ability of medical science to control disease. Man's ability to know his environment and to control and organize the natural world has always been considered one of the hallmarks of his humanity. So in the biblical creation story God brings the animals to man for him to recognize and name, and commands Adam to have dominion over what has been created. Man becomes himself by discovering and controlling his environment.

The methods and techniques of science, however, for all the knowledge and practical benefits they have brought, are not the only way in which man can become himself and enjoy the fullness of his humanity. They are only one line of human development among others. But so spectacular have been the achievements of the scientific method, and its prestige in consequence has been so great, that it has come to be popularly assumed that detached observation followed by the putting of two and two together about what is observed is the only legitimate way in which the mind can function. Reason, therefore, has come to mean no more than our ability to calculate in cold blood about a world that impinges upon our senses. In our concern to be the intellectual masters of matter and in the very success of that enterprise we have become the slaves of a certain limited concept of mind. The mind as a detached observing and calculating machine is considered omnicompetent. It is widely supposed to be progressing surely towards omniscience and omnipotence. It has in fact been invested with the attributes of God. The mind in this limited sense, however, is much more like Frankenstein. It is out of control. It can harness unlimited reserves of physical force and what will be done with them is awaited with fear.

But to see the destructive or deadening effect of mind equated with machine there is no need to call in evidence the future possibility of nuclear disaster. When, according to the general background of assumption, the mind is used as if it were no more than a calculating machine, its deadening effect becomes apparent on all sides. For life comes from personal involvement and communion with ourselves and our world. But the mental machine is concerned only with intellectual domination and possession. It kills the living reality in order to analyse it. Analyse a flower, petal by petal, and there is no flower. We murder to dissect. 'Grey cold eyes,' said Nietzsche, 'do not know the value of things.' Intellectual analysis reduces the world to a heap of dismantled machinery. Since man is popularly identified with his mental faculties and his mental faculties with their capacity to analyse and dissect, it will be useful here to give various examples of how the mind, so considered, deadens what it touches.

4

Let us suppose that in one of the quality papers we read an article on the economic condition of India. We are intellectually interested by the article but not personally moved. For what confronts us is not the living reality of suffering flesh and blood but a table of statistics linked up with a number of verbalized concepts. The economy of India can produce wealth to this or that degree. It is distributed in this or that way. The result is poverty on such and such a scale; so many people living at subsistence level, so many people below it. And so on. The usefulness of such a statistical analysis is not of course being denied. It is the necessary preliminary to improvement. What we are here concerned to point out is the difference between our perusal of the statistics and verbalized concepts in the article on the one hand, and, on the other, our reaction if these were to take flesh and be acted out in front of us. If therefore we were to claim that the article confronts us with the realities of life in India, the claim would be true only to a very limited degree and in an extremely anaemic sense. To acquire information is not to be bitten by reality.

Or suppose a musicologist attends a concert. His expertise could enable him to receive what is played with far more articulate understanding than that of the average concertgoer. But suppose he is there as a professional critic and that he is concerned to evade the impact of the music. He has gone through it often enough already and does not wish that evening to go through it again. He can protect himself against it by attending exclusively to the sheer technical virtuosity of the composer's work. He can escape from what the composer does by concentrating on how he does it. For the life and life-giving qualities of the music there has been substituted a series of mathematical arrangements, satisfying to the euclidean mind, but lacking the superabundance and creative vitality of the piece as performed. Of that, all he need notice is that the 'cellos are not up to form.

Or we could compare the work of a great novelist with the conclusions of a moral theorist. The novelist attempts to describe the experience of a person in his totality caught up in some predicament or other. The novelist's concern is to portray what Dr Leavis calls that 'delicate organic wholeness which is man's actual living in the world'. He therefore understands the immense complexity, the layer upon layer of necessary qualification, which is involved in any important moral decision. And he understands it because in some way or other he is himself living through the experience as he describes it. The moral theorist, on the other hand, is concerned not with living through what he writes about but exclusively with theory, though he will dignify theory with the name of moral principle. He applies general moral principles to specific cases in the manner of a mathematician working out a problem in logic. His final concern is not with people at all. He is arranging concepts and fitting them neatly together. What he lacks is precisely the moral experience from which his theorizing protects him. He has opted for speculating to save himself from living. Hence he is able by his moral principles to impose a totally artificial simplicity upon the actual business of making concrete moral decisions in life as it is lived. Only those, for instance, who have successfully insulated themselves from love in practice can in the abstract lay down the law with self-assurance about love in principle. We are here in a world of what Professor H. H. Price calls uncashed symbols.[2]

5

To substitute mental concepts for the living experience and so to keep the living experience at a safe distance is one of the results of equating man with mind and mind with machine. Since man is a thinking animal this has always been one of his temptations. Did not Jesus accuse the religious élite of his day of doing precisely this? They had reduced Moses and the prophets to a conceptual system safely possessed and behind this shield they protected themselves from the impact of the living God. They had their Law and they did not want its comforting security broken into by any contemporary prophetic word.

But what was always a temptation has been turned by the technological achievements of the scientific method into what claims to be a necessity. The mind as machine is presupposed to have imperial claims. What it does not know, or is incapable of knowing, is not knowledge. What does not lend itself to its method of detached observation can be taken not to exist. Yet, as scientists are well aware, this mind-machine is not simply a mirror which reflects what it observes. Science works by means of models which

[2] H. H. Price, *Belief*, Allen & Unwin, 1969, p. 402.

are not representational but mathematical. In order to grasp what is being investigated the mind-machine has to bend it to the requirements of its calculating techniques so that what is investigated conforms to the mathematical structures those techniques employ. And it is easy to conclude that what cannot thus be bent is at best dubious and most probably a delusion without meaning, let alone existence.

Hence the climate of opinion has been created that only knowledge obtained by the scientific method is reliable. Only science can be trusted to give us the real facts.

It is interesting to see how two related fields of inquiry have been influenced by this claim. The first concerns the validity of human language, the second the attempt to understand how human beings work.

The claim has been made by some philosophers that human language in order to be meaningful must be depersonalized. It must be abstracted from the people who use it and from the personal and social contexts in which it is employed. It cannot, so runs the theory, remain meaningful if it is no more than a vocal sign by means of which I as one person communicate with you as another person in a given situation. Language can be meaningful only if it is reduced to an impersonal self-contained totality. It must be a system complete in itself in which the meaning of each truth-statement can be publicly checked by reference to some sort or other of physical fact. Only thus, it has been claimed, can language be precise, consistent, verifiable, and therefore meaningful. In other words, language must be bent to the requirements of the mind-machine and the mathematical structures it employs. It is a curious claim, for language is the creation of human persons, and it was created as it was being used by persons to promote and maintain their fellowship with each other. It is difficult therefore to see how it can be self-contained, for that would make it ownerless and anonymous and thus without significance. For language surely is significant only in virtue of the people to whom it belongs. Its meaning depends upon the personal and social environment in which it is used. An impersonal language is thus a contradiction in terms unless all we wish to communicate is logical propositions, that is, some version or other of the multiplication table.

The same quest for detachment, non-involvement, objectivity, can be seen in the attempt to discover how human beings work in the field of experimental psychology. The investigations are carried out in laboratory conditions and the subject of the inquiry is human persons as so many fields of physical force. For it is only the behaviour of their bodies, their nervous or automatic reactions to various kinds of stimuli, which can be observed. The psychologist as a person is excluded from what he studies. His own feelings, his sense of self-identity, are not in any way involved. His relation to the person on whom the experiment is being made is in this context totally impersonal. The psychologist has in fact left at the laboratory door everything he is except his mind as machine. It might be thought that most of what is important about human beings has been excluded from the start. But so permeated are we with the idea that only scientific knowledge is reliable that it is a common opinion that, among the various branches of psychological study, the methods of experimental psychology alone provide us with information about human functioning which is reliable.

6

What has just been described is an attempt to reduce human language and human nature to an exact study. To this end the person pursuing the study is excluded except as a mental machine, and what is studied is depersonalized from the start. But even where exactness of anything like a comparable kind is plainly impossible, the same procedures of abstraction and depersonalization are pursued. Our implicit assumptions about the nature of our minds make us feel that they have not been properly exercised unless they have reduced what confronts them to some sort of lifeless mathematical regularity.

This is evident, to take one instance, in the talk we often hear about the necessity of rationalizing the administrative procedures we employ. The philosopher's stone of all bureaucrats is what is thus called rationalization. The bureaucrat approaches men and women as the technologist approaches the materials he organizes. The men and women cease to be regarded as persons each with his own incalculable character, needs, and aspirations, and become no more than units in a collectivity to be arranged in various patterns – the excellence of the patterns being judged according to the degree of theoretical coherence and tidiness they display. It goes without saying that there is no virtue in inefficiency as such and that efficient organization is in itself wholly desirable. But the efficiency must be directed towards allowing men and women the maximum opportunity of being fully themselves and not towards the implementation of a bureaucrat's dream. Yet in practice the two aims are often confused, and it is easy for the planners to imagine that the satisfaction of their own euclidean minds by order and neatness is the best way of serving the human interests of the people they seek to organize. And what the planners need to justify this often quite unwarrantable identification of their own satisfaction with other people's needs is all too ready to hand. Man is a rational being – i.e. he is a mind-machine, and therefore it is to his interest to be treated as a mind-machine and made to function as such in a collectivity organized for that purpose. And if the victims object to thus being rationalized, it must be because they are not yet fully rational. They have not yet understood that they are mathematical units and that therefore they can live most satisfactorily in patterns which are mathematically satisfying. Are they sentimental? Do they react emotionally to the proposed rationalization? Do they stupidly imagine that they have some kind of personal investment in the apparently haphazard contexts in which they live? Do they want to feel that they are themselves? Do they, in short, offend every single rule of scientific objectivity? Then they must be compelled to think otherwise. They cannot be allowed to continue defying the demands of reason and order.

A similar attempt at scientific objectivity is often made with regard to sexual matters. It is an example worth considering because of its universal relevance. Scientific objectivity with regard to sex has destroyed the superstitious and destructive fears sex often aroused in people. Those fears have been shown up as chimeras. It has been demonstrated that sexual activity causes neither physical nor mental deterioration. Meanwhile the realistic fear of bringing an unwanted child into the world is being removed by technology. It will not be long before contraceptive methods are a hundred per cent safe. Sex, objectively considered, and in view of reliable contraception, can thus be regarded without fear as an extremely enjoyable and entirely harmless kind of behaviour. So far the detached observations of the mind-machine have given freedom. But they have done so only by excluding a great deal of what men and women are. For with enormous strength and depth of feeling men and women spend their time searching for their own identity. And for this search to be successful they have to experience communion with another person at a very deep level – a communion involving for each of them almost all of what they are. And this is what the detached objective view of sex makes no allowance for. It has reduced what could be the means of a total experience to a scheduled and investigated commodity not unlike other kinds of consumer goods. As the young man in the *Playboy* cartoon says to the girl he is passionately embracing – 'Why speak of love at a time like this?' The result is that after intercourse people feel less themselves not more. They have been tantalized by an empty show of communion in which a seemingly promised identity has eluded them. It is not being claimed that this experience or lack of it has behind it the authority of science. The point being made is that the mind, equated with a complex of observing, calculating, and controlling functions, may come to its own valid conclusions about sex. But when, because this is regarded as the only way of knowing, those conclusions are regarded as the whole truth (since there is no other kind of knowledge), then sex from one point of view may be liberated, but only at the cost of meaninglessness. The very principle of non-involvement or objectivity, essential to the functioning of the scientific method, makes this inevitable.

*

7

And sex here is an epitome of life. If we look at the whole of our world through the same scientifically objective glasses and imagine that only by the use of these glasses can we see things which are in fact there, then our lives will be robbed of a great deal of meaning, for we shall be cut off from what we observe and our isolation from it will prevent us from finding ourselves. We shall become slaves of what we call our minds, reduced to unsatisfied and anonymous ghosts.

8

Symptoms of this condition are not absent from our society. Violence, for instance, is one of the ways in which people try to reassure themselves about their own identity. To destroy something or injure somebody is a way of showing oneself that one has acted effectively and that therefore one exists. For all its destructive effects both on victim and perpetrator, violence is still a protest against having no identity, against not being a person.

Whether or not it erupts in violence, a great deal of rebellion in the contemporary world, especially among the young, is a reaction against depersonalizing processes felt as a threat to personal being. The rebellion may hitch itself to some political cause or ideology. But frequently the political issues (even when they are a matter of local politics, like staff–student relations in a university) are no more than a convenient way of articulating a much deeper sense of grievance arising from the threat of personal diminishment or extinction. For when in the name of order and reason people are organized into patterns of living, rules of behaviour, categories of one kind or another, then they rebel against the role thus imposed upon them of being mere units in a general scheme. And their rebellion is often directed against organization as such, against the very principle of rationality and the forms of order it imposes. This has been described by Dostoevsky in his *Letters from the Underworld*: 'Man prefers to act as he wills rather than as reason and interest dictate. In only one single case does man consciously and deliberately want something absurd, and that is the silliest thing of all, *to have the right* to want the absurd and not to be bound by the necessity of wanting only what is reasonable. . . . He emphasizes his capriciousness and stupidity in order to persuade himself that people are people and not the keys of a piano.' Dostoevsky goes on to describe man's uninterrupted striving after something ahead, 'that is, *in life itself*, rather than in some end which obviously must be a static formula of the same kind as two and two make four. For two and two make four is not a part of life but the beginning of death.' If man is forced into rational moulds and his life fenced about with formulae, he 'will go mad on purpose so as to have no judgement and behave as he likes'.

The protest against rationality and the forms of order it imposes is generally blind acting out of strong unidentified feeling, but it has its roots in the quest for personal integrity. Destroy the machinery that man himself may live. In 1969, for instance, the University of Illinois had its library catalogues destroyed. On any showing this was an utterly barbaric act of vandalism. What could be achieved by thus destroying the necessary equipment of learning? Certainly not life. The only possible source for such behaviour is a blind kicking against the very principle of rationality with the ordered structures and categories it imposes. For order, arrangement, categorization, structure, are the products of the mind-machine (it was Dostoevsky who called it the euclidean mind), and when man is identified without remainder with mind so understood, he is isolated because when he uses his mind to know he has no personal investment in what he knows. He merely inspects it as from a cabin of insulating glass. And since a sense of personal identity can come only through communion with the world, what shuts off that communion is felt as a killer. It threatens to rob a person of his unique personality. A student today is an obvious example. He finds the threat we have described not only in the pursuit of his studies but in the necessarily bureaucratic structure of university organization. He is put to live in such a place. He is given a timetable which plans his day for him. These arrangements of course are designed for his good so that each student can get the best of what the university offers. But they hardly help the student to feel that he belongs. On the contrary, they make him feel no more than a coin which has to be put in the appropriate slot at the appropriate time. He feels himself a detached object who in his studies observes and learns about other detached objects. And this is experienced as murder and the murderer is identified with the rational form or order in which he is caught up. Hence form and order become themselves the embodiment of evil and have to be destroyed. The killer must himself be killed. There is no need to add that no positive or constructive result follows from any such attempt to kill the enemy. Chaos cannot be creative. But then revenge never is.

The protest against what is experienced as bringing isolation and thus personal diminishment can take the form not of rebelling against organization but of opting out of it. The hippies and flower-children, for instance, have opted out of society because they find it organized in such a way that little or no scope is given to feeling. The possibility of personal communion is, they think, at a minimum, if it exists at all. They would repudiate the notion that they are being inspired by any exacting ideal. What they want is to feel what they are, to live spontaneously, and to be free from the cerebral and rehearsed responses which the conditions of our culture make inevitable. Whether mere flight will give them what they are looking for remains doubtful. But they witness to a state of affairs in which the individual in society has lost his sense of identity because he has lost his sense of belonging. No doubt social and economic factors contribute to this – most of the hippies come from middle-class suburbia. But at the root of the matter there is the basic attitude towards reality which separates people from it – the cerebral observation which is a kind of intellectual voyeurism.

But there are other ways of gaining self-feeling which promise more immediate results than literal flight from home and city – drugs. The attraction of drugs is that they effortlessly produce feelings of personal richness and worth. People capable of describing their experience under L.S.D., for instance, testify to an expansion of consciousness in which the self is felt to be, not only in communion with its world, but merged beatifically with it. In the initial stages at least everything seems to vibrate with a glorious life which is both its own and at the same time the life of the perceiving subject. All barriers between subject and object, perceiver and perceived, seem broken down. The self is felt to be the All. Feeling is at its maximum degree of intensity. What you are is experienced as cascades and paroxysms of belonging. Self is an infinite richness. It is common knowledge that such trips usually end with reverse feelings of equal intensity. The self feels intolerably isolated in a condition of unbearable despair. The sense of infinite richness is replaced by a sense of infinite pain. The beatific vision turns into the tortures of the damned. It is also common knowledge that the use of hard drugs outside proper medical control may lead at any moment to catastrophe (like walking out of a top-storey window) and is certain once one is addicted to lead to serious illness. In view of what is not a risk but a certainty it might well seem puzzling that young people ever begin going on trips. One does not strike a match in a dark room if one knows that there is an escape of gas because the benefit of the light is outweighed by the destructive force of the inevitable explosion. People presumably take to hard drugs for a wide variety of reasons from curiosity and a desire to be with it to plainly suicidal impulses. But an important factor among others must be the bankruptcy of self-feeling. People without a sense of identity, who feel no more than isolated objects among other isolated objects, must be strongly tempted by what offers to give an experience which feels like superabundance of being, however temporary the experience is. It is the starving who eat poisoned fruit, and it is people starved of what they are who are most likely to succumb to the attractions of a trip. That is what makes the traffic in hard drugs symptomatic of our society as a whole. It is difficult to speak of marijuana in the same terms, not because it is so widely used, but because its physical effects are uncertain and they seem if anything to be less harmful than those of alcohol. But psychic dependence on either pot or gin must arise from the absence of a satisfying degree of self-feeling (often in the form of unreceptivity to self evidenced by neurotic anxiety) caused by some lack of contact and communion. It is interesting to note a parallel in a society quite different from our own. The Navaho Indians of Arizona and New Mexico used to live in closely knit communities in which the individual found his identity in that of the tribe. The tribal bonds were broken up by the American economy, leaving the individual Navaho in a state of isolation wondering who he was. He was alone without a felt environment. It is here that his condition was similar to our own. And it was in this condition of felt isolation that he began eating peyote (a cactus whose concentrate is mescaline) which 'gave him a sense of greatly enhanced personal worth'.[3] The sense of identity he once possessed in virtue of his communion with his lived environment was then given to him by the drug.

It is neither technology nor urbanization in themselves which make people uncertain who they are, but the isolation which springs from their feeling that they do not belong to a world. To the Navaho this feeling came from the break-up of his tribal life. To us the feeling of not belonging has come partly no doubt from the break-up of parallel though very much less closely knit social groupings, but chiefly from the assumption that there is only one way of knowing – that which detaches the observer from what he observes and reduces both to a lifeless abstraction. Intellectualism in this sense has always been the refuge of those who fear the contact and involvement by which alone we can live deeply and fully. It is no new phenomenon. But in our own time it has not only been given a certificate of respectability. It has come to be held indispensable to any kind of valid knowledge.

9

Life is therefore basically impoverished. The self is restricted to dismally narrow limits. Instead of using our minds to gain access

---

[3] See Mary Douglas, *Natural Symbols*, Cresset Press, 1970, pp. 12–14, 107–8. I have found her book most illuminating on the matters discussed in this section.

to realms of feeling which would unite us to our world and therefore with what we ourselves are, we allow our minds to be restricted to a narrow set of functions which claim an absolute monopoly. It is as if each of us lived on a desert island with microscopes and telescopes as our only companions. When we are not using our microscopes to observe ourselves, we can each of us see through our telescope that we are being observed by similar instruments from other desert islands. Meanwhile we are wearing germ-proof suits lest we be infected by some toxic quality emanating from what we observe.

The moment may come when our impoverishment becomes intolerable. It is then that we allow ourselves to be taken over lock, stock, and barrel by some ideology, political or religious. Separated from our own feelings, we purchase feelings ready-made from the party or the church with which we have identified ourselves. Divorced from our own personal identity, we borrow an identity from the cause we have espoused. Unable to be ourselves, we become good party members instead. For the mind has its morticians as well as the body. They are the purveyors of mental and emotional cosmetics – bottles whose content is all basically the same in that they all provide a substitute for living, but which have different smells labelled Marxism, Maoism, Christianity, Moral Rearmament, the American Way of Life, Permissiveness, the New Left, and so on. Some of these smells are considered to harmonize with each other so that they can be used together. Others are considered so contrary to each other and in such flagrant contradiction that it will be a matter of life and death that the smell you happen to have chosen or which has been chosen for you should smother or eliminate its rival. And that is the point at which the threat of nuclear catastrophe emerges. Alienated from their own inherent life, people take on a substitute for living and call it themselves. And since they identify their own particular substitute for living with life itself, they inevitably feel that their life is threatened by the claims and encroachments of other substitutes for living. Hence rival substitutes for living take each other by the throat. It used to be Catholics *versus* Protestants. Now it is Communism against

Capitalism. On a less threatening level it is the permissive society against traditional morality, or religious belief as a set of doctrinal formulae against scientific atheism. The emotional logic here is obvious. Better be sold to a prefabricated cause than to feel intolerably isolated. The ultimate enemy is inner isolation because it makes a man feel a non-person. The prefabricated cause enables us to forget the isolation. Hence the preservation of the prefabricated cause is confused with self-preservation. So the cause must be defended to our last breath. Better dead than red. Better annihilated than isolated. It is once again the issue between *eros* and *thanatos*, considered this time in terms of the battle not for the body but for the mind – supposing they can be separated, which they cannot.

10

There is no need to give further examples of the mind as death-dealing. The deadness it brings lies all about us and stares us in the face. We have become the slaves of a certain limited concept of mind, and from that slavery we need desperately to be delivered. We need to die to mind as no more than a machine for exercising intellectual mastery and taking intellectual possession. And we need to be raised up to mind as the means of personal involvement and therefore of personal enrichment. We need to discover thinking as living. That is what resurrection is in the sphere of mind.

That does not mean embarking on a Luddite bonanza making war on technology or fatuously attempting to denigrate the achievements of science. But it does mean abandoning the assumption that the way of knowing used by the scientist in his researches, however valid in its own sphere, is the only valid way of knowing. And it does mean discovering that there are different and other ways of knowing which belong at least as deeply, perhaps more deeply, to our humanity, and without whose exercise we are very much less than human.

The main characteristic of these other ways of knowing is that they lead to personal union with what is known. They expand the being of the knower so that he becomes fully himself by the felt presence with him of what he knows. There is no attempt at domination. The mind is no longer concerned to strangle reality in order to possess it. Rather the mind is recognized as a door I can open to let in my world alive, to receive the life brought, and to discover that my own life is created by it. The mind here has the function of uniting, so that I am aware of my indissoluble involvement with what I receive. It is by accepting this involvement that I grow to maturity and fulfilment. Knowing, in other words, is not separated from feeling, or thinking from experience. It is, incidentally, a state of mind familiar to the pure scientist as he contemplates some mystery to which his research has given him access.

But what then of objectivity? Is it abandoned, leaving me wallowing in private feelings totally unrelated to the public and external world? That is an obvious fear. But the fear is a liar. Objectivity is by no means abandoned. But it is an objectivity which enables me to be united with what I know rather than insulating me against it. Far from separating me from what I perceive, objectivity is here the necessary condition of union with it. For in order to be united with what I perceive I must allow it to be itself and respect its identity. I must not confuse it with my own wishes and fantasies. If I do, there will be no creative contact because there will be no contact at all. I shall be alone with my own projections, however decorative a centre-piece (to use Freud's phrase) they may appear to provide.

Here Job can be taken as an archetypal example. It was as a detached theoretician that Job was unable to make sense of the misfortunes which had befallen him. He could not square his sufferings with his theoretical fantasy of what reality was like. It was a sum in moral mathematics which would not work out. His friends thought they had solved it by reducing Job himself to theoretical dimensions. Theory required that he must somehow have been an evil man. So for the actual Job who feared God and was upright in heart they substituted a theoretical Job who was neither, a Job who was not a living man but a logical necessity. Their theory about reality required as its necessary inference a theory about Job. Job himself travelled – or was taken – in the opposite direction. He refused to abandon his experience of what he was for a *theory* of what he was. He continued to protest his integrity and uprightness even though it contradicted his theoretical fantasy about reality. Then the Lord spoke to Job out of the whirlwind. Reality was revealed to Job at first hand in all its terrifying power and ruthlessness. It was seen in its giant strength to belong to an order which smashed to pieces the theoretical cage in which Job and his friends had sought to keep it captive. In his experience of reality as it truly was in itself, and in the consequent break-up of the projection upon it of his own fantasies, Job died and was raised from the dead. There was no more querulous insistence upon the injustice of life. All was now awe and wonder at the terrifying mystery through which he had lived. It had raised him up fulfilled, although not in any sense which previously he could have imagined – 'I have spoken of great things which I have not understood, things too wonderful for me to know. I knew of thee only by report, but now I see thee with my own eyes. Therefore I melt away; I repent in dust and ashes.'[4]

Job lived a reality not very distant from that lived by the Hindu hymn-writer – 'all creation is the sport of my mad mother Kali'. It was Job the theoretician who rejected that description. And it was of his theory that Job had been the victim, not of his sufferings. For reality is at its most destructive when we attempt to protect ourselves against it behind the treacherous security of our theories. Reality faced, on the other hand, is life-enhancing even when, paradoxically, it threatens to destroy us. Kali is still our mother in the very madness of her sport. The Lord is still our God in the very ruthlessness with which he exhibits his invincible power.

[4] Job 41:3–6 (New English Bible).

But the reality we live need not be so total or dramatic as that which came to Job. It can assume many forms and can impinge upon us in varying degrees of intensity. Often it will take the form of a quiet and steady presence whose creative impact upon us will be felt as nothing out of the ordinary. But whenever the impact occurs, the mind will be a door to let life in, so that our total self is thereby enriched. And knowing will consist of union with what is known so that the mutual belonging of knower and known is established as a felt experience.

This abstract description must now be given concrete form. Examples must be taken from our ordinary daily experience. How, for instance, do we know places and people? And what has occurred when we have come to know a work of art?

12

The place which for us feels most like home is an environment with which our communion is so much a matter of course that we generally take it for granted. Yet when the biblical creation legend says that man was made of the dust of the ground, it can be taken almost literally. For our home-ground, the square miles of territory which provide our geographical context, is known by us in such a way that it contributes to what we are. It is, as we say, in our blood. If people are articulate enough they can communicate their sense of being created by where they live. We need think only of Wordsworth and the Lake District, Dickens and London, Tolstoy and the Russian countryside, Conrad and the sea, Yeats and Ireland, Arnold Bennett and the Potteries. But what writers can describe and communicate is true also of the average man who is not thus articulate. He too knows his home-ground, not as material for theory or data for statistical analysis, but as the womb which gives him birth and the air which gives him life and the food which nourishes what he is. Remove a cockney from London and we say that he is out of his element. A countryman may move to the town in search of higher wages, but he will feel the effect of being thus cut off from his roots in a diminishment of personal identity. A sailor may be given better accommodation than his hammock in a tramp steamer, but he will not feel fully himself until he goes to sea again. A Cornishman may make his money and live in the Bahamas, but he will know that for his sense of being a person he owes much more to the mother-earth of his native county than to the sun and luxury he is now in a position to afford. Such people will be able to give you a great deal of information about the places they belong to. In the hands of a competent television interviewer they will be able to tell you about its noises and smells, the kind of people there, the prevailing climate and winds, the currents or the hills and valleys with their prevailing vegetation, the sort of ships or houses or streets they live among, the standard of living among the various kinds of inhabitant. And quite a lot of this information will have been put to practical use. It will have been used to control the environment – to make a living, to grow crops, to navigate a ship, to know the corners where newspapers sell fastest, to raise a Cornish garden. But this kind of knowing – the kind which can provide information and effect control – is subordinate to a deeper more encompassing knowing which is a personal communion with what is known and creates a two-way traffic between the man who apprehends and the locality apprehended. It is the kind of knowledge implied by the phrase in the Prayer Book psalm: 'I will lift up mine eyes unto the hills from whence cometh my help.' The place known is distinct and other from the cockney or countryman or sailor or Cornishman who knows it. And yet because the place has helped to make him it has become part of what he is, so that in knowing it he also at the same time knows himself. Thus the act of knowing by which he knows his home-ground could be described as a kind of self-forgetful self-knowing, not because the distinction between place and person has been obliterated, but because place and person are in such deep communion that the place is the medium by which its inhabitant feels and knows his own identity. It is in walking down the Old Kent Road that the cockney is most certain of what he is. Yet what he sees is no mere fantasy without objective existence as he will quickly discover if he is transplanted to a

Dorsetshire village. What has been obliterated is not the distinction between place and person but the separation of knowledge from feeling, of thought from experience, of knowing from being. For the place lived in is not treated as an object to be held at arm's length in order to be inspected, but is received and accepted as an embracing reality.

13

What is true of places is *a fortiori* true of people. We know them as living presences who in the last resort elude our attempts at categorization. They are more than can be described. In the end we know them only by means of our communion with them, in terms of the common life we share with each other. And it is by means of the experience which each has of the other that the identity of each is enlarged and developed.

Let us use an imaginary instance – the same George and Margaret we mentioned in Chapter 2. George's marriage, as we saw, has made all the difference to him. A friend asks George why he is so much more alive. George says it is Margaret. 'I know that,' says the friend, 'I'm not a complete fool. But I want you to tell me what Margaret means to you. After all you went to university and got a good degree in chemistry and I would like some serious exact thinking on your part about Margaret to help me with my book on the sociology of marriage.' George tries his best and is as honest and exact as he can be. 'Well, first I find Margaret physically attractive. I enjoy having sex with her. And apart from bed, she is also beautiful. She gives me genuine aesthetic as well as sexual satisfaction. She is intelligent. She knows what my work is about and is interested in how it goes. We share a large amount of common interests which we enjoy discussing with each other – we once argued all evening about Virginia Woolf. She is marvellously sensitive and knows how I'm feeling before I tell her and warns me more often than not that she is bored stiff with my moods. She has a marvellous sense of fun – her enjoyment of life is infectious. She is superb with the kids. She is a capable manager.

She runs the house and cooks well.' The friend stops taking notes and asks after a few moments' silence, 'Is that all?' George looks puzzled. Each of the things he has said about Margaret is true, yet, listed in this way and added up, they don't begin to describe what Margaret really means to George. In fact they are almost a libel on her because she is so infinitely more than this collection of attributes ascribed to her. Bedworthy, beautiful, intelligent, sensitive, full of fun, a good mother and efficient housekeeper – each is true, but as it happens they could all be said of Mary, the doctor's wife next door, and Margaret isn't Mary, not by a long chalk. George gives up. 'The truth about Margaret,' he says, 'is that I love her.' The friend looks let down. Love is hardly suitable material for a sociological analysis. What George had attempted but failed to do was to describe Margaret with anything approaching adequacy in terms of that detached observation necessary for the scientific method. Margaret as the person who is his wife is robbed of her reality when she is submitted to this type of intellectual investigation. As a person she can be known adequately only in the mutual exchange, in the reciprocal giving and taking, of love. In his knowledge of Margaret, George cannot dissociate what he is from what Margaret is. For it is in terms of what he is as a person that he knows what Margaret is as a person, and he knows what he is as a person largely through Margaret's knowing him. The same of course is true of Margaret. In this context knowing and being known are inseparable. For knowing is the reality of communion. Knowing here is what loving means and vice versa, just as knowledge here is the product of love and vice versa. For George to know Margaret is for him to receive the mystery which she is and thereby to know himself as the mystery he is. Knowing and loving are different ways of speaking of the same act. It is the act in virtue of which we are. To know and to love is to be.

Clearly, objectivity is not absent here. George, it is true, does not know Margaret as an object. And he has discovered that the attempt to describe her as an object, or as a catalogue of objects, is futile, since it leaves out the very essence of what she is and reduces her to an unreal inventory. But George's communion with Margaret is a communion with somebody whose presence is her own inalienable identity. Margaret is herself and it is only as herself, in her otherness from George and in terms of her own inherent nature and personality, that communion with her is possible. If George mistakes what she really is for some fantasy about her and turns her into a dream-girl, then to that extent communion with her will be impossible for she will not be present to be united to. George will be confronted only with his own projections. The knowing which is loving demands the establishing of identity as its condition, the identity of the known and so of the knower – in this case of Margaret who is known and thereby of George who knows. That is why sentimentality is the enemy of personal communion. Just as the mind as an instrument for detached observation murders what it inspects in order to possess it as so many dissected pieces, so the emotions can make a similar bid for possession by reducing what touches them to a self-generated reverie in which the reality of the other disappears in a haze of false feeling. If the path of true love never did run smooth, that is because true love must ever be breaking through and breaking up the reveries which distort and obscure the real identity of the persons concerned. Truly to love somebody is truly to know them, and this involves passing well beyond both the theories in which they are frozen to death and the reveries in which they are melted down to the point of non-existence. Only when these twin temptations have been resisted will genuine communion be possible. Only then shall we know properly and well. 'A loving man is a knowing-willing man developing dimensions of his own being and of other beings, dimensions which come into being *as* he loves. His knowing in loving is a more comprehensive knowledge which tells him about himself and his fellow men even as they both *realize* their potential and fulfil each other.'[5]

[5] P. A. Bertocci, Royal Institute of Philosophy Lectures, vol. 2: *Talk of God*, Macmillan, 1969, p. 195 (his italics).

*

14

We can know a place or a person by belonging to them as they belong to us. A similar kind of knowledge is involved in all aesthetic experience. Aesthetic appreciation is not the recognition of value in a void, for that would reduce it to a mechanistic reaction like a thermometer registering heat. In aesthetic experience value is recognized in a personal context. The person of the viewer goes out to the work of art because it is experienced as expressing something – some insight, or affirmation, or faith – already possessed by the viewer, but so far only implicit and inarticulate. The work of art thus elicits the assent of the viewer who says Yes to it in a manner similar to the way in which he says Yes to the person he loves. His response to the work (as to the beloved) is a self-discovery, since in the work he finds expressed and articulated something in himself which hitherto has been only potential and dormant. His appreciation, if he is informed, will of course be critical. He will understand and admire the technique of the executant – how, if he is a painter, he has used line, colour, composition, perspective, and so on. But the viewer's admiration will not stop at how the thing has been done, exquisite though the craftsmanship may be. His final reaction will be not to how but to *what* has been done, to the finished object in its total impact.

This final reaction can be described, if only in part. It will include an experience of meeting. For the picture, even if it is a still-life or an abstract, will not be a static or passive object. It will possess a vitality which impinges upon the viewer whose concentration upon it will be met by a power emanating from it. If, we may say, it is the viewer who concentrates, it is the picture which holds his attention. Some sort of communication between them is established and it is a two-way traffic. The imagination of the artist embodied in the picture sets in motion the viewer's own imagination, and this in turn enables the viewer to see the picture in greater depth. If therefore the viewer can be said to know the picture, it is a knowledge which comes from some sort of communion between the two in which both are active. In his appreciation of the picture the viewer will be saying something like – 'Yes, that is so.' This is not of course a comment on the picture's representational fidelity to the external world (for the picture may be an abstract, and who, in any case, has ever seen Delft in the shimmering luminosity of Vermeer's painting or sea and sky in the melting colours of Archie Knox's pictures?). To say 'Yes, that is so' is to affirm some sheer power of being in what the picture embodies. It is to recognize the picture as giving expression to what magnificently *is*. What the picture embodies makes the claim 'I am', and to that claim we make some sort of total assent. By means of our contact with the power of being which is inherent in the picture our own power of being is reinforced. Hence to those sensitive to the visual arts a visit to the gallery is not entertainment, even the kind of entertainment for which we have to work hard. It is certainly a pleasure. But that is because it is a bracing experience in which we receive fresh supplies of the courage to be. From the living identity of the picture (in which the imagination of the artist has expressed something which we recognize as our own) virtue flows into us so that our own identity is thereby confirmed. What has thus been revealed may be something destructive like Goya's *Witches' Sabbath* for instance. But it makes no difference. We can still say 'Yes' to the picture. In articulating our own destructive potential and enabling us to recognize and receive it, the picture gives us life. For what stifles us is not our destructiveness but our hiding from it under covert and convenient seeming.

That in part at least is our final reaction to a work of art. If therefore aesthetic appreciation means our coming to know a work in the fullness of its value, our knowledge here is not that of a spectator. To know in this context is an act of communion between knower and known in which the knower is active in so far as he gives his whole power of concentration to the work before him, but in which he is also passive in so far as he receives from the work before him its own particular kind of enriching quality. And whatever the form, shape, texture, colour, and so on by means of which the enriching quality is articulated, the viewer is aware of a fundamental kinship between himself and what he

sees. For both are expressions of the will and power to be. Both
testify to life against death. Hence the viewer's Amen, his 'Yes,
that is so' whereby he acknowledges that he is revitalized by what
he sees, that by it his own personal being is reinforced.

15

What is true of the visual arts is true also of music. A musical
composition is not known simply in terms of its craftsmanship.
The musicologist, as we have seen, can reduce it to no more than
that if for any reason he wishes to evade its impact or has heard it
so often that it has grown stale on him. But to the receptive and
unjaded listener, musically informed though he will have to be,
the work played comes over with the power of an affirmation.
It utters a comprehensive and undeniable Yes. Even when the
composition is troubled in texture and expresses what sounds like
doubt or pain or terror or discord, those experiences, as caught
and articulated in the music, affirm themselves as life. They are
shown not as nonentity but as significance and grandeur, however costly their achievement. To know the music is to live with
it and through it. The music has to take possession of the listener
so that it becomes

> . . . music heard so deeply
> That it is not heard at all, but you are the music
> While the music lasts.[6]

Nobody can claim to know the Beethoven quartets if at their
performance he has been no more than an aural observer, supposing that to be possible.

16

If with regard to music and the visual arts the act of knowing
necessitates the personal involvement of the knower in what he
knows, the same is even more obviously true with regard to
writing. A poem, a play, or a novel can be known by us to the

[6] T. S. Eliot, 'The Dry Salvages', 5, *Four Quartets*, Faber & Faber, 1944.

extent in which the feelings they express or the predicaments they describe are recognized as our own. The power of a great work of literature consists in its capacity to point at us and say – 'Thou art the man.' Odysseus, Oedipus, Lear, Phèdre, Borkman are not illusory people who never existed. They are us. They are everyman. That this has always been known is obvious from the attention they have received. Non-people who never existed cannot excite interest, let alone retain it for centuries. It is true that in terms of our conscious selves and our social personae few of us are heroes, saints, felons, or devils. But underneath the surface of consciousness we find all these figures claiming their stake in what we are as if waiting for their chance to take command. When therefore we meet them in literature it is ourselves we meet, even if hitherto we have been unaware of our potential for being like that, and however much, once aware of it, it is a case of letting I dare not wait upon I would.

The writer can write authentically only of those experiences he himself undergoes. That means, of course, that he knows their substance not their accidents. Shakespeare, to have written *Lear*, must have experienced the brutal consequences of blind arrogance and self-deception, even though he was not a king and probably had no daughters. Racine, to have written *Phèdre*, must have known the consuming passion of self-contradictory desire even though he was not a woman in love with her stepson. The experience thus undergone will be imaginary, not in the sense that it is unreal, untrue, or non-existent, but in the literal sense that the experience is felt and known in the fullness of its reality by means of the imagination. For imagination is not only a valid way of knowing. To grasp any human situation in its depth and subtlety imagination is the *sine qua non* of knowing. Nor is imagination primarily the ability to put oneself in somebody else's shoes. It is primarily the ability to put oneself in one's own shoes and hence to realize that they belong to everybody else as well. If a playwright or novelist is able to describe his characters from the inside that is because he knows them first as himself – 'Madame Bovary is myself!' said Flaubert. Imagination consists in sensitivity to what is going on within oneself and therefore within others. And it is sensitivity to what is going on not merely on the surface of what we are but in its hitherto unknown depths. So imagination has been described as 'life coming to consciousness'.[7] It is an emerging awareness of ourselves and of the dynamics by which we operate as persons. And from this it expands to an awareness of others and of our world in general. For the writer it must always be a present awareness. His imagination must be active as he writes. It is as he writes that life comes to consciousness. If his work therefore is to live, to be revelatory of what we are, then what he describes will not be experiences remembered in tranquillity (unless his purpose is to describe that particular state of mind). As he writes he will be discovering what he describes and living through it. He will be plumbing his own capacity for joy, jealousy, doubt, fear, love, or whatever it is. 'The Dante of the *Inferno* was not a man who *had been* through hell, but a man who went into hell amaking.'[8]

To write creatively is not to spend a pleasant Sunday afternoon playing with Professor Price's uncashed symbols. It is a total receptivity to whatever comes, regardless of cost.

It is obvious therefore that to know a work of literature is much more than to know about it. To know here demands of us that we share the experience of the writer. And unless we do his work will remain a closed book to us. What the writer offers us is life, and it will be in vain unless it kindles the flame of life within ourselves. Or to put it more explicitly, the imagination of the writer sets in motion our own imagination. Life coming to consciousness in him produces the same effect in us so that the writer's initial act of creation in writing his work continues in us as we read and study it. Only then shall we begin to know it. That is why commentaries can continue to be written on works of genius. It is not necessarily that scholarship has advanced or that our technical equipment is better than that available in the past, but that the creative power of the writer embodied in his

[7] L. C. Knights, in J. Coulson (ed.), *Theology and the University*, Darton, 1964, p. 217.

[8] Saunders Lewis, in J. M. Todd (ed.), *The Arts, Artists. and Thinkers*, Longmans, Green, 1958, p. 78 (his italics).

work can continue in successive generations to generate fresh creative understanding. As the saying puts it – fresh light is for ever breaking forth from God's holy word. A work of genius speaks to every age, but what it says to each age (as to each individual) will not be precisely identical. That does not reduce knowledge of a literary work to pure subjectivism. The commentator must be sensitive to what the writer says and to what he does not say. If he fails in sensitivity here, the commentator's exposition will be worthless. The objective reference is not absent in criticism. But it is of a kind which, far from excluding the subjective response, originates it and sets it going.

The objective reference in understanding a literary work echoes an objectivity in the work itself. The work survives because it gives expression to things in human life which just are so. If the writer's vision were completely idiosyncratic, it would not even have the chance of being forgotten. His work could evoke no response. Thus 'to say that a poem is a personal utterance does not mean that it is an act of self-expression. The experience a poet endeavours to embody in a poem is an experience of reality common to all men; it is only his in that this reality is perceived from a perspective which nobody else but he can occupy'[9] – though we can, of course, share the perspective he has thus made available. Indeed, until our vision is created by his and his perception becomes our own, we shall not have begun to know his work.

17

These examples illustrate a way of knowing which all of us in fact continually use, and it is by instinct that we use it, not by deliberate choice. It is the natural way of nourishing our humanity. Knowledge as union is life. If, therefore, we look for resurrection in the sphere of mind, it is not a state of which we have no experience. The experience is there. But it remains for us to recognize it and accept its implications.

[9] W. H. Auden, *Secondary Worlds*, Faber & Faber, 1968, p. 131.

It will be seen, for instance, that all the examples given have one prominent feature in common – the absence of intellectual certainty. When we know places and people and works of art, it is not the sort of knowledge which is susceptible to proof or demonstration. Perhaps we shall consider certainty too big a sacrifice to make for life. If so, then we must exclude ourselves from knowledge as union, for intellectual certainty is what it can never provide.

For what we know remains ultimately mysterious. We can establish communion with it as a felt experience in which its own otherness is retained, but neither in fact nor in principle can we reduce it to the size of our capacity to sum it up. If we could, the possibility of communion would be excluded, for what we should have before us would be a sum of our own mental or verbal concepts, not the living substance of the thing itself. Places, people, and works of art allow us to share their life with them. But they remain intellectually elusive. Our act of knowing does not pin them down in a definition. They transcend all description and explanation. They are always more than anything we can say or think about them. The fact that they thus pass beyond the range of our capacity to describe or explain them may leave us feeling insecure about them. So we are confronted with the choice – insecurity or life? For without knowledge as communion our humanity is starved. We become uncertain of our identity and begin to wonder who we are. Yet the temptation remains strong to try to banish insecurity by attempting intellectual certainty. We seek to abandon knowledge as communion for the knowledge which reduces what it apprehends to concepts which can be logically dissected and drawn up into patterns of logical coherence, thus taking away from the reality described the very life which makes it what it is. When all knowledge is considered a matter of such intellectual mastery and possession there may indeed be certainty but it is certainty about shadows and shades. For what we are certain of is the concepts and formulae in our head and not the reality in its living power. From communion with the reality we have shut ourselves off in the cause of certainty. Hence our personal impoverishment. We are isolated from the very world which as material for intellectual investigation and analysis we are possessing more and more. The words of Jesus are startlingly true here as in other connections – 'A man's life consisteth not in the abundance of the things which he possesseth.'[10] That includes intellectual possessions. 'And what,' he asked, 'shall it profit a man if he gains the whole world and forfeits his life?'[11] That is precisely the prospect of those who are obsessed to the exclusion of all else by knowledge as possession and its ultimately empty certainties. They are dying of bankruptcy in the midst of the paper money they have accumulated. And they need, if anyone does, to be raised from the dead.

18

The achievements of science and technology have given unique prestige to knowledge as possession. But it was possible in all civilized communities in all ages to evade communion with reality by the claim to possess it as theoretical and conceptual truth. We noticed Job and his friends doing so and also the religious élite in the time of Jesus. We also saw how the musicologist and the moral theorist can easily evade the reality with which they are supposed to be concerned.

Knowledge as intellectual possession does not in itself bring personal impoverishment. On the contrary, such knowledge, by enabling us to understand the uniformities of nature and thus enabling us to control it or to adjust ourselves accordingly, is the *sine qua non* of even the most elementary civilization. And in the last hundred years it has delivered us from a great deal of crippling fear and has brought us freedom and power. And it is knowledge as intellectual possession which gives us conceptual access to worlds which are not our immediate concern and of which therefore we can have no direct personal experience. Indeed knowledge as possession may be the first elementary step to knowledge as communion. I have to get to know about a work of art as the first stage of getting to know it. The astronomer's

[10] Luke 12:15.   [11] Mark 8:36.

instruments have first to discover the universe before he can contemplate it with wonder and loving awe.

Personal impoverishment arises not from knowledge as possession but from the exclusive claims we make for it as if it were the only valid way of knowing. When such exclusive claims are made, it is because we are frightened of the insecurity which knowledge as communion involves. For in the last resort communion of this kind can be only with unfathomable mystery, and our inability fully to understand may make us acutely uneasy. The compensatory obverse of this fear is the pride of riches. We allay our fears by equating ourselves with what we possess. Riches, however, invariably cut us off from life, and knowledge as possession (when it stops there) cuts us off from the reality it claims to be knowledge of. It is perhaps the most important sense in which it is hard for a rich man to enter the kingdom of God. He trusts in his accumulated mental constructs and mistakes them for reality. And allied to all this there may be sheer spiritual sloth – an unwillingness to allow reality to impinge upon us because of the trouble it will cause. We may be too lazy to take our bearings afresh. We may not want to reorientate ourselves. We may not want, in the real sense, to repent. It is easier to continue working vigorously in the old rut, keeping the mind energizing as a machine for taking what is real out of reality. In a number of ways we may have a vested interest in excluding mystery and the demands it makes on us. So we claim that there is no mystery, that nothing in principle is mysterious.

In the end we find ourselves each on his own desert island, dressed in our insulating suits, identified with our observing instruments, exorcized indeed of superstition but a tempting target for seven other devils worse than the first. For it is intolerable to live without self-feeling, with no sense of identity. And it is thus that our very germ-proof suits become the breeding ground of an ideology.

The price of life, however, is invariably death. We have to die in order to live. The rich man has to become poor if he is not to be sent empty away. The poor little rich man who boasts himself in the extent of his intellectual wealth has to learn the meaning of poverty and nakedness. The man organized against his own insecurity has to expose himself to it. The man who lusts after intellectual certainty has to accept the pain of intellectual doubt. The counters with which he spends his time happily playing have to be exchanged for the realities they are supposed to represent. The symbols have to be cashed. If he is to live a fully human life, he has to be born again so that he may know the truth of the paradox that it is in having nothing that we possess all things. For to live means dying to the world as the intellectual possession of our closed-up ego in order to rediscover it by meeting and communing with it. And if we find that the world still belongs to us after all, that is because we have now realized that we belong to it. It is the theme of Shakespeare's *Timon* – 'Nothing brings me all things.' 'How blest,' said Jesus, 'are they who know that they are poor.'[12]

19

The way of knowing as communion is the natural way of nourishing our humanity. Because it is natural it is also spiritual. For man in his totality, in his comprehensive unity of body-mind, is spiritual. The Eternal Word is for ever becoming flesh as man's developing self in its entirety is continually being called into being. If the impoverished man who trusts for security in what his mind dominates and possesses is to give place to the man who finds life in the knowledge which is communion, that death and resurrection can occur only because he has heard the voice of the Eternal Word. To hear that creative Word is the authentic spiritual experience by which we are made alive. And life-giving spiritual experience is not one department of life nor one activity among others, but the whole of life in its creative impact upon us as we open ourselves to receive it. To take the examples given – when a place or a person or a work of art communicates with us and elicits our own capacity for communion with it, then we have heard the voice of the Eternal Word. It is a spiritual experience which began when we were in our cradle and responded inarticulately to our mother's love. And it continues as our world

12 Matthew 5:3 (New English Bible).

summons us to respond to it by going out to meet it. The place where we feel most at home, the people we most deeply love, the works of genius which have most fired our imagination, these are instances of the Word being made flesh and dwelling among us, and thus creating us. Each of these instances confronts us with its own mystery. We cannot fully describe or explain any of them. It is in being themselves that they beckon us to communion with them and their final identity is intellectually elusive. If we know them deeply (as we can) we shall hear them say, '*Noli me tangere.*' We shall recognize that they have about them an inviolability which means that a condition of thus knowing them deeply is our acceptance with regard to them of a fundamental unknowing. If we try to overcome this necessity of unknowing by attempting to force our way into their ultimate secret and insisting that they hand over their mystery for dissection, then the place, the people, the work of art, disappear altogether and leave us with no more than an inventory of disjointed fragments.

> He who binds to himself a joy
> Does the wingèd life destroy;
> But he who kisses the joy as it flies
> Lives in eternity's sun rise.[13]

Blake here has caught to perfection the difference between the two ways of knowing, and the impossibility of communion with what we have forcibly made into our own intellectual property. To recognize and respect the mystery in all things, to discover thereby that we belong to them as they belong to us, to find our own identity in this experience of intercourse with what is potentially inclusive of all reality, that is to hear the voice of the Eternal Word and to be raised up to fullness of life.

20

One of the things which hinders us from perceiving this is the tendency of all religions to substitute knowledge as possession for

---

[13] *The Complete Writings of William Blake*, edited by Geoffrey Keynes, Oxford University Press, 1966, p. 179.

knowledge as communion. The founder's direct awareness of mystery and participation is felt to be too elusive to survive, and also too exacting in the spiritual sensitivity it demands. So the direct awareness of mystery and the command to watch is solidified into creeds, orthodoxies, and conventional ascetic practices. The orthodoxies can be intellectually possessed (like that possessed by Job's friends), and they call not for watchfulness but for submission, not for sensitivity but for capitulation. Instead of the challenge to discover reality and in communing with it to find life, we are presented with a list of truths for our intellectual assent. Or to put the same thing in a favourite biblical idiom, instead of being confronted by the living word of the Lord God, we are asked to believe ecclesiastical statements of one sort or another about him. Instead of being made aware of the mystery which surrounds us at all times and in all places, we are presented with the mystery processed and packaged in a collection of verbalized concepts which by their very nature have abstracted what is real from the realities they set out to describe. And since the devout assume that they possess the truth in the verbalized concepts to which they subscribe, what is called their faith generally makes them insensitive to reality as it is revealed all around them, and deaf to the Eternal Word speaking through all things. For they must ever be cutting it down to size, squeezing it out of shape, emptying it of content, so as to make it square with their particular orthodoxy. A Buddhist, for instance, has written – 'The Buddha's teaching was a mode of living, a method of approach to life itself. Buddhism is man's attempt to create a cage for this experience, and to the extent that he succeeds he fails to inherit the Wisdom which the Master offered to mankind.'[14]

Must not the same be said of Christians and Jesus? The concern of Jesus was for the present moment – 'Sufficient unto the day is the evil thereof.' ('Pull out the arrow,' said the Buddha, 'and do not delay with inquiries as to its length and provenance, nor the name and tribe of the man who shot it.') And what Jesus gave us

[14] Christmas Humphreys, *Buddhism*, Penguin Books, 1951, p. 61.

were not doctrines but parables. (As did the Buddha.) The appeal of the parables is to the imagination. Their purpose is to challenge their listeners into awareness of a mystery which permeates the whole of life and shows itself forth on all sides – in a farmer sowing, in a woman baking, in a thief committing robbery with violence, in a generous employer, in a conscientious shepherd, in a dishonest agent, in a loquacious old lady, in a forgiving father, in a strict master from whom his servants can expect no gratitude, in a man who let money stagnate, in a king who punishes a beggar for not wearing a morning suit at a royal wedding, in houses built on suitable or unsuitable land. Jesus told these stories to elicit the sensitivity of his listeners to the ultimate meaning and challenge of life. And the story form indicates that the meaning is beyond the cognizance of the intellect-bound mind. It can be apprehended only intuitively, imaginatively, as the life of the listener comes to consciousness. Of course generations of commentators have attempted to decode the parables, claiming to interpret their meaning in abstract terms. But in so doing they have either reduced them to false and boring allegories or confined them within the limits of some doctrinal strait-waistcoat claiming that they are all ways of making the same point or announcing the same event. Such attempts at decoding are symptomatic. They indicate the transformation of knowledge as communion with mystery into knowledge as the possession of truths. If today the Christian churches are unable to nourish men with the bread of life (so that they are looking for it in the East), it is because the church very early on sold itself to rigid conceptualization, claiming to be the repository of truth (Irenaeus – 180 – called the church a truth bank), reducing everything in heaven and on earth to its own dismally parochial boundaries and equating the Eternal Word with its own cult-idol and the particular systems of beliefs which fasten it to the wall.

Mercifully, however, illusion can ever be the medium of reality. The features of the Eternal Word can begin to be discerned in those of the cult-idol. Along with the church's claim to possess the truth there has also been from very early times a protest against the claim, a recognition that knowledge as possession is here impossible and we must either have knowledge as communion or nothing at all. Hence the insistence that God can be spoken of only in negative terms, or the attempts to try out the possibilities of paradoxical language about him, or the intricacies of the way of analogy. The mystics have always stressed the necessity of the negative way until with St John of the Cross *todo* is apprehended as *nada*, fullness as emptiness. Three representative instances can be taken of this denial of knowledge as possession:

St Gregory of Nyssa (330–95): 'The true vision and the true knowledge of what we seek consists precisely in not seeing, in an awareness that our God transcends all knowledge and is everywhere cut off from us by the darkness of incomprehensibility.' Eckhart (1260–1327): 'I pray God to deliver me from God.' And in our own day there was the similar – though widely misunderstood – protest of Bonhoeffer: 'There is no God of whom we can say "there is a God"', and 'Now that it has come of age the world is more godless, and perhaps it is for that very reason nearer to God than before.'

The churches, if they are to lead men to what gives them life, cannot evade the necessity of death and resurrection in this sphere as in all others. They must be prepared to die to the claim that they possess the truth in their doctrinal conceptualizations, in order to be raised up as witnesses to mystery which can be known only by means of knowledge as communion. In the Johannine idiom, having communion with the Eternal Word is *doing* the truth, living in it, and only so can men have life and have it more abundantly. This, surely, is the true oecumenism – not the attempt to fit one set of doctrines into another set, but the willingness to become aware of the beckoning mystery of life everywhere, of which doctrinal statements are no more than the solidified sediment. If the *experience* of a Catholic, a Protestant, a Jew, a Hindu, a Buddhist, a Moslem, is similar or identical – and as described by their wisest and holiest men they manifestly are[15] – then of what importance is the fact that the doctrinal cages in which each

---

[15] cf. Evelyn Underhill, *Mysticism*, Methuen, 1930, pp. 86–7.

tradition has sought to hold the experience captive are made of different designs and in different metals? The intellect-bound mind sets up barriers which are illusory. And the barriers are not only between one religion and another. They can often separate the believer from the purity and fullness of his own experience.

> Then my delivered soul herself shall learn
> A darker knowledge and in hatred turn
> From every thought of God mankind has had.
> Thought is a garment and the soul's a bride
> That cannot in that trash and tinsel hide:
> Hatred of God may bring the soul to God.[16]

But perhaps we have been too severe on doctrinal conceptualizations, emphasizing too exclusively their destructive and suffocating qualities. If so, it is because they have been taken too much *au pied de la lettre* as if mystery could be handed out as information. They have, after all, kept Christendom divided with each church claiming its own information as more correct than that of others. If doctrines could be treated as a form of parable, then they might point to the reality they inevitably obscure when they are taken as descriptions. There is much to be said for the views here of W. H. Auden: 'Dogmatic theological statements are to be comprehended neither as logical propositions nor as poetic utterances: they are to be taken rather as shaggy-dog stories: they have a point, but he who tries too hard to get it will miss it.'[17] Or in the more seemly words of the Bishop of Durham: 'Other disciplines will be judged primarily on the quality of their articulation; theology will be judged primarily on its ability to point to mystery. The only distinctive function theology can or need claim is that of being the guardian and spokesman of insight and mystery.'[18] This was the road being trod by Thomas Merton, the Cistercian monk, towards the end of his life, as is evident from

[16] W. B. Yeats, 'Supernatural Songs', 5, *The Collected Poems, of W.B. Yeats,* Macmillan, 1950.

[17] Auden, *Secondary Worlds*, p. 136.

[18] I. T. Ramsey, *Models and Mystery*, Oxford University Press, 1964, p. 61.

his attestation as a Catholic Christian: 'I intend to become as good a Buddhist as I can . . . I am a Hindu.'[19]

When our knowledge is knowledge as communion, we have no need to be led into any esoteric land in order to be confronted with the mystery of the Eternal Word. It is to be found in what creates us, and what creates us lies round about us. The bread of life is our daily bread, and it nourishes us by being eaten not inspected.

Perhaps the argument of this chapter can find a fitting summary in Shakespeare's last play. In his later plays 'he had come to believe that reasons should be obedient to the imagination – or to imaginative love as some would prefer to call it'. When, in *The Tempest*, Ariel is given his freedom, it is freedom to bring the power of imagination to bear upon his familiar environment:

> Where the bee sucks, there suck I,
> In a cowslip's bell I lie;
> Merrily, merrily, shall I live now
> Under the blossom that hangs on the bough.

Ariel 'will not use his freedom to fly away to some distant heaven: he will hide under the nearest flower. The world of spirit, in other words, is not Another World after all. It is this world rightly seen and heard. . . . Shakespeare is telling us that sense and spirit are as much made for each other as lovers are. It is appetite and intellect that have put an abyss between them.'[20]

Resurrection of mind and body is one.

[19] Thomas Merton, in *Monastic Studies*, New York, No. 7 (Michaelmas 1969), p. 10.

[20] H. C. Goddard, *The Meaning of Shakespeare*, vol. 2, University of Chicago Press, 1968, pp. 269 et seq.

CHAPTER FOUR

RESURRECTION & GOODNESS

I

I_F the body or mind is isolated from the rest of what we are, it is reduced to a state of ultimate frustration. From this living death it can be raised up by the creative call of the Eternal Word mediated through the common circumstances of life. Our living in the world, we could say, has the power to create us. But this miracle of resurrection does not occur necessarily or automatically. For our living in the world, instead of creating us may, on the contrary, keep us permanently dead.

2

Our world in the sense of the people among whom we live consists of a number of societies – family, job, class, country – to which we find ourselves belonging. And our relation to these societies is always double-edged. For the societies to which we belong can be both life-giving and death-dealing. On the one hand they can elicit from us what we are, and by creating us can make us creative. When this happens the society and its traditions transmit to us what might be called the living past. But, on the other hand, there can come a point where the society which so far has given us life may hinder our further development by preventing us from growing out of the role it has assigned to us and passing beyond it. For what societies tend to require of us is that we should be satisfactory members of them. If we are not satisfactory members, or our growth as persons has made us less so than we once were, the society will exercise various pressures to make us conform to type. When this happens the societies become the gaolers of what we shall call the dead (or undead) past.

3

We can see this clearly in the archetypal society of the family. There is no need to describe its life-giving qualities. We all owe to it (or its equivalent) whatever creative capacities we possess. It was by its means that we developed confidence in ourselves and became capable of standing on our own feet. But that is only half the story. For the family can often also inhibit growth and prevent us from being or becoming what we are. In all the various kinds of family relationships the demand can be made that we be no more than satisfactory members of the society concerned, that we should equate living with playing the particular role required of us.

Husbands or wives, for instance, sometimes demand of their spouses that their personal identity be wholly monopolized by their matrimonial role – or else. A young child will try to insist that his mother be no more than his mother, that her role as his mother monopolize everything she is. And to effect this result the child will attempt to levy all kinds of emotional blackmail. Parents in their turn can make the same sort of demands upon their children. They can construct prefabricated roles for their children to play. Sons or daughters must behave in the right way, be interested in the right things, hold the right views, adopt the right attitudes, as though they existed to boost their parents' self-esteem by being good advertisements for them: 'Our son tells us everything'; 'He never minds if the better man wins'; 'Our daughter would never think of allowing her boy-friends to go too far'; 'She likes staying home in the evening'; 'Our children know they are free to choose for themselves.' Even when parents are not so foolish as to betray themselves by uttering such sentiments explicitly, the sentiments can be tacitly assumed and emotional pressures organized to effect the desired results. In so far as children succumb to the pressures, their growth as persons is stunted. They learn to play a role rather than to become themselves.

It is common knowledge and experience enough that the society of the family can be one of the most suffocating kind. In such circumstances the worst off are those unaware of their bondage because with them living has been completely identified with playing a part. We could say that their only experience of life is death, and so they accept their deadness as the natural order of things. Instead of living to create, they exist to conform. To conform is for them the *summum bonum*, and not to conform is the ultimate evil. They do not realize that they have been robbed of their identity. For they have been conditioned by emotional pressures to feel guilty at the very suggestion that they should break out of their role and be themselves instead. That way, they have come instinctively to imagine, lies wickedness and retribution.

4

This family murder is the archetypal murder committed by all societies in so far as their main concern is to constrict us within the limits of being their satisfactory members. It can occur in connection with any of the communities in which we are caught up. The murder takes different forms according to the community concerned, but its results are always the same – obedience to the demand for conformity so that, instead of being and becoming ourselves, we remain adequate performers of the role assigned to us.

A man may be a rebel, for instance, because he has fire in his belly and wishes to change what he considers wrong with the world. If so, in his rebellion he is being and becoming himself. But rebellion can be no more than the enactment of a role or a counter-role. As counter-role it is a reaction against the attempted imposition of roles in childhood. Or a man may find himself caught up in a community where rebellion is expected of him. Then it is a role. It is as a rebel that he is accepted and valued. In these circumstances rebellion is a mode of conformity. It is by playing the part of a rebel that he purchases membership of the group. But he seldom sees the trick which has been played upon him. He sincerely believes he is on fire for the cause. And he is content that for the sake of the cause his humanity should wither away. Zeal is invariably the index of fabricated or false identity. It is the conformist who is the most zealous, since he has to disguise his non-entity from himself. 'Men who are not free always idealize their bondage,' is Pasternak's comment on Yuri Zhivago's revolutionary enthusiasm.

The role of rebel is often exchanged eventually for the role of establishment man. Here again a distinction must be made. If a society has made possible the growth and flowering of a man's abilities and personality, then his attempts to preserve the structure of his *alma mater* are the means whereby he is and becomes himself. But people can be strong establishment men in order to feel that they belong to its élite. They are pillars of society in order precisely to feel that they are pillars. They murder their essential self because they feel more secure as impressive brass. Unable to be through love in communion with their world, they have opted for exercising power over it. And the price of power is conformity to the attitudes and conventions of the society concerned. It is true of many men that high office somehow dehumanizes them. That is because, without being aware of it, they have sought high office precisely in order to be dehumanized. Unable to trust the apparently frail living substance of their own flesh, they have sought to be turned into a pillar of society, and they are reassured to know that the pillar is the man. It is not that they consider conforming to the particular conventions concerned a price worth paying. They are unaware of paying it.

> Let him not cease to praise
> Then, his spacious days;
> Yes, and the success
> Let him bless, let him bless:
> Let him see in this
> The profit larger
> And the sin venial,
> Lest he see as it is
> The loss as major
> And final, final.[1]

The community which claims our conformity may be the permissive society. The paradox is only apparent. Compelling us to be free is an old trick – worked out at its most tragically farcical among devotees of Marxism-Leninism. It is, of course, by totally

---

[1] W. H. Auden, 'His Excellency', *Collected Shorter Poems, 1927–1957*, Faber & Faber, 1966.

different methods that the permissive society seeks to compel us to be free, and the freedom it would impose is of a different kind. What is identical is the demand for conformity as the price of belonging. Freedom in the context of permissiveness is equated with instant instinctual satisfaction. Its god is the body as machine, and his worshippers, like the worshippers of all false gods, are intent on making converts. Not to be permissive in this sense is held to be a sign of weakness, prejudice, fear, of not being switched on. It is thus that the blackmail to conform operates. And those who allow themselves to be victimized by it abandon their personal identity in order to play the part of a bag of instincts, rather like an actor on the stage dressed up to represent a grotesque, except that the actor does not confuse himself with his costume or role. To be a satisfactory member of the permissive society can involve the denial of personal identity to an excruciating degree: 'A girl student slept with her boy-friend, who also slept with other girls. They discussed these incidents in great detail. The language they used, as fashion demanded, was that of pimps and prostitutes. The code that governed their behaviour was reminiscent of that of Red Indians being tortured at the stake; honour required that, however great the agony, not a muscle must twitch.'[2]

Social conformity in the narrow snobbish sense of keeping up with the Joneses is a source of so much amusement that it seems unfair to discuss it seriously. In so far as it amuses us, we are not of course its victims. Laughter is always a sign of freedom. But people can and do equate their personal value with their prestige possessions, which can include not only inanimate objects but also whoever in the particular context are held to constitute the smart set. When this equation is made, the person making it feels that in himself he does not exist, that in himself he is the little man who isn't there. It is therefore necessary for him to assert – 'I am my house in the country or my new car or the top people I know.' In so far as his prestige possessions are people, in order to make and keep their acquaintance he has to adapt himself to their outlook

[2] A. Mitscherlich, *Society without the Father, a Contribution to Social Psychology*, translated by E. Mosbacher, Tavistock Publications, 1969, p. 216.

and presuppositions in the effort to be one of them instead of himself. A performance of this kind, if it is kept up, eventually persuades the performer that he is in fact what he is pretending to be, and he thus disappears totally into the false identity he has assumed. His reactions can never be genuinely spontaneous. They are conditioned by the character he has chosen to play. When he says – 'This is what I think', what he means is – 'This is what somebody who knew Professor Einstein and Madame Curie is bound to think.' In so far as it is inanimate objects which provide our prestige possessions, the role we have been persuaded to play is an economic one. We are functioning as satisfactory members of our economic society. Today in the West the economy depends upon a fairly rapid degree of consumption. Spending sprees and so on help consumption to keep pace with production. It is production which provides the mass of the people with their livelihood, and unless there is a market for what is produced, factories close and there is unemployment. In this context the advertising industry is seen to exercise a very necessary function. In persuading us to buy commodities it is providing employment for those who make them. But the advertising industry can do this only by creating a certain degree of false identity in the people it persuades. Its aim is to make them imagine that they cannot be fully themselves without acquiring the consumer goods advertised. When the trick succeeds, people confuse what they are with the commodities they buy, so that without the fitted carpet, the new car, the with-it suit, they feel less than themselves. They have been brainwashed into being satisfactory members of their economic society.

It is not so easy to speak of the society of the nation as here in Britain we have lost our sense of national identity, as is evidenced by the efforts of Scottish and Welsh nationalists to create one of their own. But across the water in Northern Ireland, we see what being a satisfactory member of a national society can involve. The conflict in Ulster is between two nations, two national identities, and in order to qualify as a true-hearted citizen of either nation, one has, to put it mildly, to lose a certain degree of one's humanity. The pressures brought to bear on individuals to abandon their own personal identity in order to conform to the prejudices and phobias of the two respective national groups is obviously enormous. And it is not a case of individuals being forced to do what they do not want to do (though that must often be so). What happens is that individuals are successfully persuaded that they are Ulstermen or Irishmen first and people second. A man feels that he just is his nation.

5

But that, we say, is the result of history. It is an illuminating platitude. For it highlights the fact that we are all from one point of view the products of historical necessity. We are all the products of the various environments into which we were born, and each of those environments is linked by a causal chain to the depths of the past. In this sense each of us has had an infinitely long history before he begins living in the world at all. Each of the societies to which we find ourselves belonging is conditioned by forces – genetic, economic, political, cultural – stretching back to the dawn of time. And when those societies in their turn condition us, they are the instruments by which the past makes its bid to possess us. In so far as a society prevents us from achieving our full human stature by insisting that our personal identity be confined within the limits it sets, then to that degree it is effectively making us the prisoners of the past. And the past is dead (or rather it is undead in the sense we have described). That is our predicament as persons. We need society in order to develop into our full humanity. But the societies to which we perforce belong are conditioned by the dead (or undead) past. And by belonging to them we become their captives. We are constrained to confine our identity within the limits set for us. By persuading or brainwashing us into being no more than their satisfactory members, the societies implement the hold of the past over us. 'The whole weight of the past,' said Marx, 'lies like a mountain on the brain of the living.' His diagnosis here agrees with that of Christian orthodoxy. For when it is said that we are conceived and born in sin, or that we are dead in trespasses and sins, the statements can be understood to refer to our being thus conditioned by the past of the human race, that we have little or no freedom to be our true selves. What, however, Marx saw more clearly than Christian orthodoxy is that this state of affairs is not our fault but our tragedy. The game we play is the result of the game which has been and is being played on us. For Marx, capitalist exploiters were not guilty men. They were the agents or victims of objective social and economic laws of which they were unconscious. To indulge, therefore, in ecstasies of guilt and sorrow for sin (as we have been led to believe good Christians should) is not merely irrelevant. It is the final trick the past plays on us to keep us its slaves. For it diverts us from our real task of unloosing our chains by actually changing the situation. Of course the conventional Christian apologist will answer that our guilt-laden sorrow is not for original but actual or personal sin – not for the state of affairs into which we were born but for what we ourselves do or fail to do. The distinction is neat enough in theory. But how as conditioned beings do we in practice distinguish between the two? In any case (the basis here of Marx's argument) guilt is most often aroused by *not* conforming to the predetermined patterns in which the past enslaves us. Freud adds to Marx's argument by showing how infantile fantasies of omnipotence lead us fantastically to overrate the power of our feelings and actions, and how our sense of guilt attributes to them positively world-shattering strength, so that in consequence we are immobilized by our fears and the past continues to exercise its deadly dominion over us. To this slavery, as Marx saw, the churches contribute handsomely by their emphasis on sin and guilt – an example of corruption which is almost laughable in its clarity and completeness, since penitence and forgiveness are meant to set us free from the past so that we may orientate ourselves afresh. Seldom are aim and result in such total contradiction.

One thing is certain. We cannot be raised up from the dead past by any trick that past may play upon us.

But a distinction already made could here bear repeating. In so far as the past has provided us with the means to attain our freedom and find our full identity, we are, of course, in its debt. So, for instance, if in Britain we have freedom of speech and of the press, that has its roots in the past development of our parliamentary democracy. If we cannot be imprisoned without trial, that has its roots in the past establishment of the rule of law. To inveigh against the past as such would be not only absurd but mischievously destructive. We have to distinguish between the past as life-giving and the past as death-dealing. If we here ignore the past as life-giving, that is not because we are unaware of our fundamental debt to it, but because it poses no problem save that of the need for perpetual vigilance. Our concern here therefore is with the past in so far as, in the ways we have illustrated, it hinders or prevents our full development as responsible persons. That is what we mean by the dead or undead past.

From that dead or undead past, we cannot be raised up by any trick it plays upon us. If we are stunted in our growth as persons by the societies which demand that we should be no more than satisfactory members of them, then we cannot get out of our predicament by becoming members of yet another society making similar demands. Salvation, in other words, cannot be by the way of conformity. We cannot find ourselves by playing a part.

6

The tragedy of religion as organized in the Christian (and no doubt other) churches is that in practice this is precisely what it often asks us to do. In theory, of course, it is held that if there is a conflict between the dictates of private conscience and those of ecclesiastical authority, then a man must follow his own conscience. The trouble is that the churches seldom build up personal identity enough for this conflict to occur. The recent rebellion among Roman Catholics against the Pope's pronouncement on the contraceptive pill might seem like a notable exception. But that does not look so much like a rebellion of churchmen as churchmen as a rebellion of churchmen as the inheritors of a liberal tradition of secular culture. The rebellion is not, for instance, much in evidence in Eire or Latin America. It is easy here for non-Romans to adopt a more-enlightened-than-thou attitude.

It is true that the non-Roman churches have a looser structure of authority and that they do not lay down explicit detailed rules of conduct. But then neither do the societies we described above – the rebel society, the establishment society, the permissive society, the economic society. The stunting conformity these societies impose upon their victims is not effected by anything so crude as a published set of rules. They exercise their influence subtly by generating their own particular atmosphere of longing and offered satisfaction. The strength of their appeal is the implication that they possess what gives life if only people would come and buy it. The non-authoritarian churches make a similar appeal, though more explicitly – they possess the secret of life and love if only people would stop being themselves and conform to the standards of truth and goodness offered. The churches, for instance, hold in esteem as a man of faith not somebody (like Jesus upon the cross) racked by the pain of tormenting doubt yet somehow still holding on, but the man who lives happily at ease with whatever are the contemporary official doctrinal formulations. And they esteem as a man of goodness not somebody (like Jesus) who challenges the ethical values and standards accepted as normative, but the man whose moral vision is confined within their limits, and who thus extols and advertises them. For all the talk about conscience, loyalty to truth and so on, what in fact the churches usually want to make people into is satisfactory conforming members of their society. And this is in essence the same old murder we have considered in this chapter from the start. If, for instance, on television, a Christian tries to describe the insights which have come to him at great cost through much toil, sweat, and blood, and these do not square exactly (as in their nature they cannot) with the official line, churchmen give vent to howls of execration, the church press is full of letters and editorials of protest, and the post-bag of the Christian concerned is full of the vituperation and abuse of which churchmen, with iron-curtain party members, appear to be the world's experts. The church, like the party, apparently possesses the truth as a branded product and the duty of its members is to sell it. When *Honest to God* sold instead (to take one example) it was like being at a play written by St John the Evangelist, with churchmen saying among themselves and to their leaders: 'Perceive ye how ye prevail nothing? Behold, the world has gone after him.' From that time on its author became a marked man like any party deviationist. The freedom of the individual to discover and grow into his own inalienable identity and thus to live and do the truth is generally paid no more than lip-service.

It is not being denied that the society of the church (like the society of the state) transmits much of the past as life-giving. The church makes accessible, for instance, the accounts of their experience given by those who have refused to accept life at second-hand and have fought and found their way to authenticity like Jesus in the wilderness, in the synagogue, in the temple, in Gethsemane, and upon the cross. It puts before us the example of men and women who have grown to their full stature by living and being the truth they have discovered. It proclaims a gospel of resurrection confronting us with the possibility of dying to our dead past so that we may live in freedom, open to the fulfilling potentialities of the future.

The church must also be given its due credit for building the tombs of the prophets – perhaps the most risky thing it does.

At the same time, however, the church remains the instrument of that same dead past from which it offers to deliver us. As we saw in the last chapter, the church has never really broken its habit of regarding its knowledge as possession. And the counterpart of this claim to possess the truth is the parallel claim to possess the forms of goodness in the official norms and values to which it asks its members to conform: 'If you want life, you must be like this and this and this and this. This is what goodness means. For this and this and this and this are always right.' Thus is goodness confused with conformity and evil with the failure or refusal to conform. In the last resort we are being asked to enact a role, to play a part, to be satisfactory members of the society – at the cost of failing to find life, let alone having it more abundantly. 'The church and Christians have throughout the ages done their best to insist on the static nature of human beings and society, to require a fixed standard of human behaviour . . . and to impose belief and morality without respect to human rights and values.'[3]

The essence of human life, however, is to be creative. To say that man is made in the image of God is to say that man shares with his creator in the work of creation. To say that the image is soiled or tarnished is to say that man has lost to some extent his ability to be creative because he has become enslaved to a dead past of some kind so that instead of creating he conforms. The remedy for this state of affairs cannot possibly be the adoption of a new pattern of conformity, however exalted and sublime may be the prefabricated values offered for imitation. Living goodness, in other words, must be the result of renewed creativity, and it will manifest itself not in terms of realizing values which exist already in some changeless ideal realm above and beyond man, but in terms of actually creating values which are new. 'The task of ethics is not to draw up a list of traditional moral norms, but to have the daring to make creative valuations.'[4] And values can thus be created only by being lived, not by being argued about or assented to. This creation of new values means that for us to enter eternity and be given eternal life is not to be raised up to the vision of some static state of changeless perfection, but to participate more and more actively in the creative processes we find all around us here and now. To share God's life is to find ourselves creating with him. To be raised from the dead by the creative call of the Eternal Word is to find that we are ourselves agents of resurrection. And to be ourselves agents of resurrection, raising men from enslavement to their own dead past, is the true meaning of ethical behaviour. Goodness, in other words, is the expression of superabundant life. It is our way of endlessly becoming more and more of what we are, so that other people are enabled to do so also. It is the overflowing of joy – the joy which brings life to everybody it meets.

Jesus, it is universally admitted, taught no general moral principles. He once used a contemporary summary of the Law – Love God and neighbour – when asked what was the most important

[3] D. L. Mumby, in *Lambeth Essays on Faith*, S.P.C.K., 1969, pp. 106–7.
[4] N. Berdyaev, *The Destiny of Man*, Geoffrey Bles, 1937, p. 20.

commandment. But otherwise his ethical teaching consisted of so many concrete examples of how the power of resurrection could be brought to bear on people in whatever strait-jacket they happened to be. Did a man's deadness impel him to take his revenge on life by striking you on the cheek? Then turn to him the other cheek as well. Did his deadness lead him to assert alleged rights over your shirt and begin suing you for it? Then give him your coat as well. Did a petty tyrant seek satisfaction by forcing you to go one mile? Then go with him two. Did a ne'er-do-well take you for a fool who could be tricked into giving or lending him money? Then give it to him without more ado. If a man curses you, return him benevolence. If he treats you badly, treat him well. To be raised from the dead is to be no longer the prisoner of one's environment. It is to be free from the chains of one's conditioning, past or present. It is to realize that it is not necessary to play the game which is being played on us, so that we can play our own game not the one imposed. That is the secret so far unlearnt by those who despitefully use us. They react to life as life has treated them. They are bloody because life is bloody. Our refusal to play their game may be for them the beginning of a discovery – that like us they are free to be their own master and to live their own life, and not to be merely the sport and toy of circumstance, with everything they do automatically dictated by what is done to them. That such behaviour is to share with God in his work of creation, to participate actively in the creative processes all around us, is explicitly stated by Jesus: 'Love your enemies and pray for those who persecute you, that you may be the sons of your Father who is in heaven; for he makes his sun to rise on the evil and on the good, and sends his rain on the just and the unjust.'[5]

It is the man raised up from his own dead past who is able by what he is to raise up others from theirs. That is what goodness means. That is the first and final principle of ethics. Ethical behaviour is not submitting to a scale of values. It is magnificently and gloriously to *be*, and in being to create. Ethical behaviour is thus the result of miracle (like resurrection of body and mind

[5] Matthew 5:44, 45.

which are the same thing regarded from a different standpoint),
and it is a miracle which at sundry times and in divers manners
happens to almost everybody.

7

One of the results of this miracle of resurrection is an ability
actually to alter the past – to change what so far has been a dead
past into a living past. Do not Christians in the light of resurrection call that Friday good? But to avoid preconceptions, let us tell
a new and imaginary tale.

Conditioned by my temperament and circumstances, I once
did Richard a serious injury. In consequence he cut himself off
from me. (This tale is not an allegory.) He became in this sense the
prisoner of what I did to him. And the day on which I did it
remained for both of us a black death-dealing day. But somehow
Richard found life. That was, I thought, clear from the novel he
published and from what I heard about the happiness of his
second marriage.

Unexpectedly – after all those years – he came to see me one
Saturday afternoon, obviously wanting to re-establish contact
with me. Inevitably I was badly put out. I felt extremely nervous,
and I was also angry with him for coming. We always hate the
people we've injured and feel it is they who have done an injury
to us, which in a sense is true; if they hadn't been there or allowed
us to injure them, we shouldn't be so undead ourselves. Anyhow
Richard called on me, and although it was only five o'clock I gave
him some whisky because I thought he must need it – that is, I
wanted some myself. I congratulated him on his novel and asked
after his new wife. Then I asked him if he had much of a garden
where he was now living. 'An acre,' he said, and went on immediately – 'You know that you ruined my career as a journalist by
that very dirty trick you played on me? For a time I was absolutely
obsessed by my hatred for you and anger. I couldn't sleep or
concentrate on anything. Then, slowly, I found other interests.
Bit by bit I was able to dismiss you from my mind. In the end you
no longer troubled me at all because you didn't exist as far as I was
concerned. As you probably know I eventually got a job at a

publisher's. I discovered you didn't exist for me when it occurred to me that I'd walked down Fleet Street twice the previous week without thinking of you. Well, thank God, I thought. It's good to know that for me he's dead and buried. But the last year or two I've found great happiness (I'll tell you about that another time). And I began to think of you again. I discovered by chance that the house I'd recently bought was only fifteen or twenty miles from where you are living. I was still aware of the injury you did me – Christ, it was hellish – and I realized that my life would certainly have been easier, less bloody complicated, less of an ordeal really, if you hadn't done it. Yet my new happiness made me feel that it wasn't so important after all. It came to me too that you must have been in pretty bloody hell yourself to have acted like that. Then I discovered that I had a very high regard for you – a real regard, I mean, not sentimental, noble, or patronising or the sort of thing our parson talks about – "do you love the neighbour whose dog shits on your front lawn?" (he thinks he's emancipated) – I said a real regard.'

Whatever injuries or blessings the past had brought him, Richard hadn't changed in one respect. Whisky always gave him an endless flow of words.

'I realized,' he went on, 'that you were somebody good, great. And I wanted to meet you again. It's odd, isn't it, that if one says anything, the opposite is also always true? When you kicked me in the balls in Fleet Street, people said that your second name had always been Judas, that you were always betraying your friends; that what you did to me was absolutely in character. And they were right. But they were wrong as well. You acted in character. You also acted out of it. You always somewhere had a very deep and sincere regard for fidelity. And I feel now that I more than half deserved what you gave me. I was an awful prig in those days and there is nothing like moral conceit to make a man blind and insensitive. Anyhow would you be willing to call it quits, so that we can start seeing something of each other again? I'd like you to meet Rosemary, my new wife.'

I promised to drive over to dinner with Richard the following week. I would have promised anything to get him out of the house. After years and years, breaking in on me without warning and raving on like one of the madder characters in Dostoevsky. It was crazy to give him whisky, but then I needed it myself. I wouldn't go to dinner.

I spent the rest of the day thinking about what he'd said. I couldn't settle down to anything else. My wife had died ten years before and our only child was grown up and married. I had been living a rather lonely life, but I had adapted myself more or less to circumstances. I wasn't in all respects satisfied with the adaptation – who ever is? – but it was tolerable. Yes, that was it, tolerable. I'd settled down and grown used to it. Of course now Richard's visit would upset the equilibrium. It would destroy my peace of mind. Why? I wonder. It wasn't being reminded of the injury I'd done him. I'd grown used to that years before. I think his visit will make me feel discontented with my adaptation to the world. 'You must slowly adapt yourself,' our doctor had said when my wife had died. Now I was already discontented. I sensed new possibilities of living, like the man who's gone sailing is bored with a steamer, or the man who's visited Chatsworth is irritated by the municipal gardens. I had thought of life, I suppose, as a matter of cutting one's losses, accepting the inevitable, and living with as little pain as possible. Richard's visit made me feel that that was no longer good enough. Why couldn't he have left me alone? Well, I suppose I hadn't when I kicked him. He meant what he said, that was clear enough. He wasn't being in the least pious. He was right about his having been a prig. But he wasn't now. He was more like a raving lunatic. I suppose I'd better go to dinner. He'll only be round here again if I don't.

I went. It wasn't half as bad as I thought it would be. I liked Rosemary. How much had he told her? You couldn't tell really, she was a bit of a Mona Lisa. I went over quite often as it turned out. I once had them to dinner here, and Rosemary was polite about my cooking – polite with a touch of pity she couldn't hide. The more I saw of Richard the clearer I became that he wasn't pretending when he said I was a great person – he always was a bit of a bloody fool.

Our renewed contact has made life much richer for me, quite

exciting in fact. You know what matchmakers women always are. Well, Rosemary threw a widow woman at my head. After four or five months we thought: 'Why the hell not?' Me and Daphne (God, what a name!) I mean. We're going to be married next week. That's why I'm a bit over-excited and spurting all this out.

When I come to think of it, the oddest thing of all is that injury I did Richard. There's no doubt it was nasty, a very dirty trick as he said. And my having done it often made me feel I'd somehow opted for death rather than life. I did it six years before my wife died, and while she was still alive I could escape myself by looking after her. It was after her death that it came home to roost. Biting your friend like that, it's the action of a desperate, terrified animal at bay. That's why I began isolating myself from people. But now, since Richard's visit, which made me so angry at the time, the injury I did him has begun to look quite different. You won't believe me, but it has become a bond between us. It's a piece of the past we have in common. It's something we've lived through together. And it's brought us both life.

Richard said he'd discovered something important about himself and the world when he found his high regard for me returning and he wanted to meet me again. When we were once more on intimate terms, he said something about its showing him what freedom was (I remember his words because they were so odd): freedom, he said, meant that, although nature was red in tooth and claw, the wolf would dwell with the lamb and a little child shall lead them. I never could understand him in one of his abstracted moods. He seemed to talk nonsense. He can't really expect Daphne to have a child at her age. But then, as I said, he was always a bit of a fool.

As for me, I don't think it would have been at all the same if I'd never done Richard the wrong. It was like getting a friend back from the dead, you see, especially coming after my wife had died. And look at the end result – a sour-tongued crusty widower of sixty-two who kept himself to himself is about to be a bridegroom. Shall I tell Daphne what I did to Richard? Probably not. But I shall always think of it when I look at her.

So much for our tale. It will have done its job if it does no more than hint of how resurrection alters the past and changes it from a past which is death-dealing to a past which is life-giving.

8

Ethics as resurrection answers the valid Marxist criticism of religion that it has no concern for changing the state of affairs and making things better. Marx saw in the Christianity of his day a machine for the production of piety and resignation. What was sincerely considered as the upholding of eternal values was in fact, he thought, a disguise for keeping things as they were so that the stranglehold of the dead past might be effectively maintained, however many people continued needlessly to suffer in consequence. The infallible instrument here, as we have seen, was the inculcation of a deep sense of guilt. For once you have made people feel guilty enough, they welcome suffering as a relief. So Christianity was presented as a pattern of conformity. Failure to conform evoked guilt for which suffering was a palliative. Forgiveness was offered if you accepted your suffering as just, and purposed amendment of life, i.e. that you sincerely promised to try harder to conform. Thus the structure of society, with all its unnecessary evils, was left to continue as before with Christianity giving it the blessing of the gods.

Marx's picture of Christianity was, of course, one-sided. It ignored Christians – in England alone, Elizabeth Fry, Wilberforce, Shaftesbury, Maurice – who devoted themselves to action aimed at changing the situation. But there was enough truth in the picture for Camus in the middle of the twentieth century to say that man 'now launches the essential undertaking of rebellion, which is that of replacing the reign of grace by the reign of justice'.[6] Camus here is thinking chiefly of the tendency among Christians to glorify suffering for its own sake even when it is at other people's expense. Marx was right again in so far as religiously devout people who are politically right wing can still be

[6] Albert Camus, *The Rebel*, translated by Anthony Bower, Hamish Hamilton, 1953, p. 46.

outraged when bishops show a concern for social righteousness and complain that they are stupidly interfering in politics; or in so far as Labour leaders, if they wish to stigmatize anything as hopelessly unrealistic and doctrinaire, call it theology. There is still a general background of feeling that Christianity is not concerned to make an impact upon the structures of society, whatever bishops and other Christian leaders say or do.

But this is inevitable when goodness is considered as conformity to pre-established norms and values. For it seems – and indeed it would be – ridiculously conceited to imagine that we were more righteous than our grandfathers and that what was good enough for them is not good enough for us. Why is it now unethical to treat Africans as the best of our grandfathers did? Have we more concern for justice and mercy than Albert Schweitzer? Why is it now unethical to starve strikers into working? Did not St Paul say: 'If any one will not work, let him not eat'?[7] Are we more moral than St Paul? God forbid. Why is capital punishment now considered by many Christians as unethical when our Christian forefathers considered it the law of God? Are we really nearer to God than they? Why has remarriage after divorce now under certain circumstances earned the blessing of the church, when it was once considered utterly wrong in all circumstances? Why was contraception wrong in 1920 and right now? Why have we now a Christian duty to keep all children at school until they are sixteen and to provide university places for all intelligent young people whatever their economic background? There is no mention of that in the Ten Commandments. Were our grandfathers less socially responsible than ourselves, less ready to give to every man his due? Can it really be supposed that we are more concerned than they were for the eternal ideals of truth, justice, mercy, and love, or that we know more about those ideals than they did?

But in social as in individual matters, ethical behaviour or goodness is not conformity to an existing value or the attempt to articulate an existing value. Ethical behaviour or goodness is resurrection. It is bringing creative insight to bear upon a social

[7] 2 Thessalonians 3:10.

situation so that whatever in that situation is deadening to human development may be changed into something life-giving. Goodness is the fruit of imagination, the product of life coming to consciousness, and this can happen only in the now and with regard to contemporary situations. What is morally right for a society is not a static unchangeable standard, but something which, because it is alive, grows and changes as fresh social situations call forth fresh creative valuations. Ethical insight as resurrection is like leaven working in dough. It ferments in society, giving it life by continually bringing about the conditions in which people may have the maximum opportunity to find and be themselves – people, that is, as they are now today.

The creative insight is generally called forth as a protest against a state of affairs which has come to be seen as death-dealing. It is generally by means of the protest against what is destructive and wrong that people come to see what is creative and right. 'In the long run, situations which are unworthy of man give rise to explicit protest, not in the name of a concept of what would here and now at the time have been worthy of man – a concept already positively defined – but in the name of human values still being sought, and which are revealed in a negative manner, i.e. in those destructive situations which evoke by contrast the values concerned.'[8]

Where in Britain at the moment we desperately need both the protest and the new moral valuations it calls forth is in the whole business of industrial relations which have become death-dealing to all concerned, not only economically but morally and spiritually. The utter uselessness here of merely applying a moral norm has been proved beyond contradiction. It is useless from any preconceived valuations to say: 'This is right. This is wrong.' For both management and workers have real grievances and can bring strong arguments to support the justice of their claims. The truth is we have not yet discovered what right and wrong mean in the context of industrial relations and we are waiting for a prophet to be raised up to show us.

This situation in our own day underlines forcibly how ethical

[8] E. Schillebeeckx, O.P., *God the Future of Man*, Sheed & Ward, 1969, p. 191.

insight and behaviour must be a matter of creativity and resurrection and cannot be a matter of conformity. 'There is no right way to organize things in this world – no way which might last for ever and be definitive. Instead, in relation to the whole, everything "right" is merely a road which must be travelled to reveal what the word "right" could not mean at the outset.'[9] If anybody doubts this, let him remember that St Paul wrote to the Corinthians: 'Were you a slave when called? Never mind', though they were to accept freedom if it was offered (7:21); and that he sent back a runaway slave to his master (Philemon) even if he exhorted the master to treat him as 'more than a slave', though he did not ask for his emancipation in the legal sense. And we must not forget that it was on board a slaver that John Newton wrote 'How sweet the name of Jesus sounds'. People who inveigh against what they describe as situational ethics seldom realize the backlash of their own criticisms. For if ethics were not situational in the sense at least which we have described, we might now be claiming the divine sanction of Christianity for the most barbarous and inhuman régimes imaginable.

9

The path of goodness, in the realm of personal and social ethics, is not the path of security or assurance. Because goodness has to be created and not applied, it involves risk and uncertainty. We can often be far from sure that what we are doing is morally right. We have to have the courage to stand out against the generally accepted opinion in the knowledge that we may well be mistaken. But risk, after all, is the price of creation as, we may say, God himself discovered. If we insist at all times on complete moral certainty, goodness becomes evil. Instead of being living and creative, goodness becomes static and destructive. That is why goodness often has such a bad name. We have all met people who are good in the worst sense of the word. Hence the people who rebel against the good can often be the people who bring about

[9] Karl Jaspers, *Nietzsche and Christianity*, Henry Regnery Company, 1961, p. 59.

the realization of new forms of goodness. Many Christians, for instance, now understand marriage much more in terms of a personal relation than in terms of contract. That is what 'right' here is coming to mean. But the pioneers of this view, with its implications for divorce and remarriage, brought down upon themselves the anathemas of almost all good Christian people. They were accused of lowering Christ's standards (as though he had been a married man whose marriage had broken down). 'Blessed are ye when men shall revile you and persecute you, and say all manner of evil against you falsely, for my sake. Rejoice and be exceeding glad: for great is your reward in heaven: for so persecuted they the prophets which were before you.'[10]

In Brieux's play *The Three Daughters of Monsieur Dupont* there is a deeply moving conflict between goodness as creativity and goodness as conformity, in which, as often in human life, goodness as conformity wins. The characters are enmeshed in the make-believe world of a standard morality. The third daughter, Julie, tries to break free and leave the husband she has never loved and who has never loved her. But the social pressures are too great and she gives up the attempt. The final curtain comes down on unforgettable lines:

MONSIEUR DUPONT (the old father): Ah my children, everything comes right when once you make up your mind to be like the rest of the world.
JULIE: Yes, like the rest of the world. I dreamed of something better. But it seems it was impossible.[11]

Pseudo-goodness, said Thomas Merton, the Cistercian monk, in the last book he wrote, 'will prefer routine duty to courage and creativity. In the end it will be content with established procedures and safe formulas, while turning a blind eye to the greatest enormities of injustice and uncharity. Such are the routines of piety that sacrifice everything else to preserve the comforts of the

[10] Matthew 5:11, 12.
[11] Eugène Brieux, *The Three Daughters of Monsieur Dupont*, Jonathan Cape.

past, however inadequate and shameful they may be in the present. Meditation, in such a case, becomes a factory for alibis, and instead of struggling with the sense of falsity and inauthenticity in oneself, it battles against the exigencies of the present with platitudes minted in the previous century. If necessary it also fabricates condemnations and denunciations of those who risk new ideas and new solutions.'[12]

If the agents of resurrection to others must first themselves be lifted up from the dead past, they must not be surprised to find it means being lifted up upon a cross. After all, they have been warned.

10

If, however, goodness is the continuing miracle of resurrection whereby we are creative because we are ourselves being created, then how comes the miracle? It was the question we had to ask before in connection with resurrection of body and mind. As we then saw, there can be no question of recipes and prescriptions. For what they can produce is only conformity not resurrection. 'The wind bloweth where it listeth and thou hearest the sound thereof but canst not tell whence it cometh or whither it goeth. So also is every one who is born of the Spirit.'[13] Yet, as we said earlier in this chapter, resurrection as creative goodness is the kind of miracle of which most people have experience in some way or other because it is mediated by ordinary people and things. The sacramental elements of the miracle are the everyday world in which we live. As Petru Dumitriu says in his great novel *Incognito*: 'A miracle is an everyday event which brings us into direct contact with the meaning of the world, and of God. If we are conscious of the divine nature of every happening and every fact, then everything is miraculous. But it is hard not to forget. Consciousness flags in its perception of the divinity of the world, and we disregard the miraculous by taking it for granted. For

[12] Thomas Merton, *The Climate of Monastic Prayer*, Irish University Press, 1969, p. 140.
[13] John 3:8.

those who worship God every event is a sign, and there are some signs which cannot be ignored.'[14]

It is clear from his novel that Dumitriu denies being a Christian. His discovery of the divinity of the world, of the divine nature of every happening and every fact, is his own self-discovery. Yet thereby (he is a Rumanian) he has lived through and made his own a characteristic insight from the living past of the Eastern Orthodox tradition which 'knows nothing of "pure nature" to which grace is added as a supernatural gift, since grace is implied in the act of creation itself'.[15]

It is in the world that we find God. It is in our communion with everything about us that we discover the resurrection and the life and are made new. But our eyes must be open to perceive it.

For the contrary is also true; which is only another way of saying that we are often blind. For as blind men we are the victims of those death-dealing qualities by which the world as our total past persistently conditions us. We have seen how that past exercises its power by means of the societies in which we live, and their inevitable tendency to diminish our identity as persons and to stunt our growth. We therefore need resurrection as a continuing miracle. We need perpetually to be receiving our sight. We need daily and hourly to be raised up again to creativity and goodness. We need every moment to be created. There is no The End in human life from which point we automatically live happily ever after. For every End is a new beginning.

Dostoevsky has put this before us with penetrating simplicity in the final pages of *Crime and Punishment*. The novel's main character, Raskolnikov, a would-be intellectual, is serving a long sentence in Siberia for murder, a murder he committed under the influence of certain theoretical notions about the freedom of a superman to do anything. It was as a theorist and in conformity with theory that he became a murderer. His past experience in St

[14] Petru Dumitriu, *Incognito*, translated by Norman Denny, Collins, 1964, p. 445.

[15] V. Lossky, *The Mystical Theology of the Eastern Church*, James Clarke, 1957, p. 101.

Petersburg and his present experience in Siberia have deadened his faculties, numbed his sensitivity, and reduced him to little more than an isolated impervious object. From this death he is raised to life again by the faithful love of Sonia, a one-time prostitute. Sonia's love for Raskolnikov finally breaks through all the defences and repressions by which, so far, he has successfully adapted himself to his exile, and thereby blocked his love for her. The miracle occurs, and his love for Sonia comes flooding into his heart. In being able now thus to receive love and to give it, Raskolnikov is made new. On the actual day of the miracle 'he even fancied that all the convicts who had been his enemies looked at him differently; he had even entered into talk with them and they answered him in a friendly way. He remembered that now, and thought it was bound to be so. Wasn't everything now bound to be changed? . . . He could not think for long together of anything that evening, and he could not have analysed anything consciously; he was simply feeling. Life had stepped into the place of theory and something quite different would work itself out in his mind.' He had seven more years of his sentence to serve – '*only* seven years. At the beginning of their happiness at some moments they were both ready to look on those seven years as though they were seven days. He did not know that the new life would not be given him for nothing, that he would have to pay dearly for it, that it would cost him great striving, great suffering. But that is the beginning of a new story. . .'[16]

It is the story with which we shall be concerned in the next chapter.

[16] Fyodor Dostoevsky, *Crime and Punishment*, translated by Constance Garnett, Heinemann, 1967, p. 482.

CHAPTER FIVE

RESURRECTION
& SUFFERING

THE past, as we have seen, can be death-dealing. As prisoners of the past our personal identity is diminished or destroyed. The gaolers we have so far considered are the various societies to which we find ourselves belonging. But the past often shackles us with an individual private gaoler of our own – the suffering which at one time or another comes to each of us. Of whatever kind our suffering may be, it is the effect of causes which lie deep in the past. Suffering is the way in which the past as death-dealing impinges upon us most immediately and most intensely.

Suffering therefore destroys. When it is severe and prolonged it can kill some essential part of us so that we cease to be anything like the people we were. And it does this in a particularly cruel way. For we are never so aware of our separate individuality as when we suffer. Suffering always involves an aloneness, a being cut off from others. Here we are with our pain – physical or mental – and for the rest of the world it is business as usual. While all our human resources are being press-ganged by the dead weight of suffering, other people are laughing, drinking in the pub, making love, planning tomorrow's picnic. Suffering excludes us from life in the very act of draining it from us. As Prince Myshkin, with characteristic perceptiveness, says to a young man in advanced consumption – 'Pass us by, and forgive us our happiness.'

Because suffering is death-dealing, it should always as far as possible be prevented. Jesus went about curing disease, and when the time of his own suffering drew near, he was human and humble enough to ask to be spared from it – 'Father, if it be possible, let this cup pass from me.' Christians have not always followed him here. They have, it is true, invariably gone out to alleviate suffering. Many of the saints have shown compassion in its most practical form. St Catherine of Genoa (1477–1510), for instance, can be considered as the founder of modern hospital work. And her concern for the sick and those in distress was typically Christian.

But, on the whole, Christians have been more eager to alleviate suffering than to prevent it. That is partly because they have tended to ally themselves with – or at least to accept – the political and economic status quo. (That in these days their politics tend to be leftish is no exception to the rule but only another instance of it.) At the back of their minds there has also often been a vague notion that suffering is God's will for man, and that when a man suffers he is receiving no more than what is justly due to him. So, for instance, in the collect for the fourth Sunday in Lent we describe ourselves as those 'who for our evil deeds do worthily deserve to be punished'. Most of all, the anticipation of eternal bliss in heaven has seemed to compensate infinitely for even the worst miseries and tortures men may have to endure on earth. Dostoevsky has given a delicious skit of this last view in the story of the man who had to walk a quadrillion kilometres in agony before he reached the gates of Paradise. But when he had passed through them, 'before he had been there two seconds, he cried out that those two seconds were worth walking not a quadrillion kilometres but a quadrillion of quadrillions, raised to the quadrillionth power! In fact, he sang "hosannah" and overdid it so, that some persons there wouldn't shake hands with him at first – he'd become too rapidly reactionary, they said.'[1]

The notion of punishment for sin and still more the expectation of heavenly bliss has led Christians passively to accept suffering on earth as inevitable and has often made them incapable of taking tragedy tragically. They have often been blind to what Walter Stein has called 'the absolute *reality* of tragic destruction',[2] and it was, as he says, the Enlightenment of the eighteenth century and the liberalism of the nineteenth (we could add the communism of the twentieth) which 're-channelled Christianity's arrested responsiveness to bare earthly destruction'.[3] There is something refreshing in the sheer common-sense of J. S. Mill's words: 'All

[1] Fyodor Dostoevsky, *The Brothers Karamazov*, translated by Constance Garnett, Heinemann, 1968, p. 683.

[2] Walter Stein, *Criticism as Dialogue*, Cambridge University Press, 1969, p. 237.

[3] Ibid.

the ground sources of human suffering are, in great degree, many of them almost entirely, conquerable by human care and effort.' Or in the terser words of Brecht: 'The sufferings of this man appal me because they are unnecessary.'

2

Whatever may be said about suffering in this chapter, let it first be clearly understood that it is a destroyer of mankind, and that where by due thought and planning it can be avoided, it should be at all costs.

It remains true, however, that while new political and economic societies may be better than their predecessors, they inevitably become the breeding-grounds of new corruptions which bring back the sufferings the new society was intended at the start permanently to eliminate. Human beings cannot so easily break with the total past of the race. And apart altogether from the structures of society, men and women remain vulnerable to sickness, catastrophe, and death, not to mention those appalling mental and emotional agonies which are the price we have to pay for being alive at all. No new society can make us proof against the savage cruelty of bereavement, the pangs of despised love, the tortures of jealousy, the despair of being locked away with only a half or quarter of what we are.

To say that suffering in some form or other is inevitably part of our human lot is not to give a charter to resigned passivity. It is to face the facts.

But here an important distinction must be observed. Facing the facts is not at all the same thing as explaining them. Allowing ourselves to be confronted with reality is not at all the same thing as theorizing about it. Indeed explanation and theorizing become often a form of escape. As Proust says, 'The habit thinking prevents us at times from feeling reality, makes us immune to it, makes it seem no more than another thought.'[4] We could say that

---

[4] Marcel Proust, *The Sweet Cheat Gone*, penultimate volume of *Remembrance of Things Past*, English edition, Chatto & Windus, 1925.

explaining facts is an attempt to soften their impact upon us. For the explanation is felt as a sort of exorcism which casts out some at least of the sheer brutality of the fact. It is thus that we escape from life into theory, from experience into doctrine, from the thing itself into talk about it.

Suffering has inevitably been given the full treatment in this respect. For being the harshest fact man has to face, it has called forth perpetual streams of explanation. The volumes of theory about suffering are endless.

The Christian tradition here is no exception. The brute fact of suffering has been continually surrounded by doctrines which endeavour to relieve it by explaining it. We must look quickly at the explanations provided. We shall see how at their own level of theory they are far from loyal to the logic they themselves demand. We shall also see how the explanation, as well as providing the comfort of apparent rational coherence (for those who wish to be persuaded), also provides illicit under-the-counter comfort of an extremely dubious kind. None of this, incidentally, need worry us. Our concern is with resurrection, and resurrection is experienced miracle. It is not explanation or theory.

3

For traditional Christian doctrine the fact of suffering imposes the most acute intellectual difficulty – the greatest difficulty with which any theory ever has to contend – that of attempting to reconcile a logical contradiction. For Christians are committed to belief in one all-powerful God of supreme goodness. And on this level of theory the question is bound to arise – if God is all-powerful, if it is he who made us and not we ourselves, then must he not be responsible for the suffering which destroys us? But if he is, then how can we maintain our belief in his supreme goodness? Somehow the Christian explanation of suffering has had to wriggle out of that logical impasse. How has it been done?

It has been done first by disregarding the fact that a great deal of human misery is due to purely natural causes – earthquake, floods, famine, disease, and death. These having been cleared out of the way, we concentrate on such suffering as can be plausibly held to be the result of human wrong-doing. And if it is asked why man is capable in the first place of wrong-doing, the answer is that without the capacity to choose the evil man could not possess free-will. He would be an automaton.

But this, although widely believed, is simply not the case. To begin with, when we appear to choose the evil, it is extremely difficult to assess the degree of our personal culpability. For we enter this world as already highly conditioned beings – conceived and born in sin, as the Christian formula has it – and the evil that we do seems often no more than the inescapable result of the evil which has first been done to us. If a man is born blind, it is not his fault that he cannot see. In the second place, the ability to choose the wrong, far from being essential to freedom, is in fact an impairment of it. The ancient Greek fathers saw this. To be perfectly free, they said, our choice must be governed entirely by what we ourselves are. It must be the expression of our own nature. If our choice is governed by what is external to ourselves, by something outside us which attracts or compels us, then we are considerably less than free. So, for instance, St Maximus the Confessor (580–662) declared freedom of choice to be a manifest limitation and imperfection, 'A perfect nature has no need of choice, for it knows naturally what is good.' And even St Augustine described the final freedom of the blessed in heaven as the inability to sin. Freedom, in short, does not consist in the ability to choose what is wrong but in the ability fully to be what we are. Hence without the ability to choose the evil we should have been more free not less. As a parallel here we could take responsiveness to music. If I am musical I cannot help responding to the power of Beethoven's quartets. But my response is not automatic. I am not thereby turned into a machine. The contrary is the case. For in responding to the quartets I experience a depth of freedom which is generally inaccessible – my response enabling me fully to be my musical self. In the same way, my being musical will make me impervious to the cheap charms of Tosti's music. Yet in being unable to respond to the music of Tosti's *Good-bye* or *Parted*, I shall not have become an automaton. It is simply that these songs provide me with no opportunity of being my musical self. If for sensitivity to music you substitute sensitivity to goodness, it will be clear that if we had been unable to choose evil, we should have been not less free than we are but more.

It was the recognition of this fact which led some Christian thinkers to excogitate the idea of a pre-mundane fall – i.e. that a spanner had been thrown into the cosmic works before man arrived on the scene at all. But this does not solve the problem. It merely pushes it a step backwards. For if our troubles are due to Satan, how came this fallen angel to lose his own musical ear?

If we want to soften the brute fact of suffering by explanation, then on this level of theory we should have the courage of our own logic. If God is the all-powerful creator and men are destroyed by suffering, then it is God, not man, who is in the dock and needs to be justified.

But another theoretical escape has been thought up. If pushing the problem of evil backwards to a time before men appeared on the scene does not solve the essential problem, then what about pushing it forwards into the future? Can we not say that the sufferings of mankind in this present world are preparing the way for, leading up to, the perfect harmony and bliss which will be ours hereafter?

It was the sheer dishonesty of this type of apologetic, its sheer disloyalty to the plain facts of human experience, which fired the wrath of Ivan Karamazov. People say that suffering is all right because God is bringing everything towards an eventual harmony and bliss which will last for ever. But, objects Ivan, if all must suffer to pay for the eternal harmony, why is it necessary to force innocent children into the scheme? 'A poor child of five was subjected to every possible torture by her cultivated parents. They beat her, thrashed her, kicked her for no reason till her body was one bruise. Then they went to greater refinements of cruelty – shut her up all night in the cold and frost in a privy.' The final harmony 'is not worth the tears of one tortured child who beats itself on the breast with its little fist and prays in its stinking outhouse, with its unexpiated tears, to "dear kind God"! It's not worth it. . . . If the sufferings of children go to swell the sum of sufferings which was necessary to pay for the truth, then I protest that the truth is not worth such a price. . . . I don't want harmony. For love for humanity I don't want it. . . . And so I hasten to give back my entrance ticket, and if I am an honest man I am bound to give it back as soon as possible. And that I am doing. It's not God I don't accept, only I most respectfully return him the ticket.'⁵

Yet it is not really odd that Christians should so easily be satisfied with the sort of apologetic which consists of little more than the easy speeches which comfort cruel men. For one of the ways in which suffering destroys us is to make us hate ourselves. I hate my pain.⁶ But since I have to live with it, I have to find some sort of *modus vivendi* with it. This I do by identifying myself with the pain, by, so to speak, taking the pain's side. For if I can feel that I am in some way an ally of the pain which is destroying me, then to that extent at least I can feel alive. But if I seek life by taking the side of the destructive pain, I can do so only by despising and hating the me which the pain is destroying. So what begins as my hatred of my pain, in time turns into my hatred of me, in the sheer attempt to live with my pain and at the same time to preserve some sort of identity. Hence I can come to welcome suffering because it provides me with the means of implementing my hatred of myself, for it is only in thus hating myself that I feel I can preserve some shreds of what I am. In such a condition it is good news indeed that suffering is the will of God, that it is just, that for our evil deeds we worthily deserve to be punished. And from here it is an easy step to conclude that what I have accepted almost joyfully as true of myself must also be true of mankind as a whole. If I suffer because I deserve it, then all men suffer because they deserve it. This indeed has often been considered as the first essential stage by means of which the joy of the everlasting gospel becomes available to us. And if by this time my destructive suffering has left me with a glimmer of moral sensibility, I can satisfy it by the easy notion that God will make everything up in the end

⁵ Dostoevsky, *The Brothers Karamazov*, p. 251.
⁶ Pain, it should be remembered, can be mental as well as physical, and mental pain is probably far commoner than physical.

by giving us all the eternal bliss of heaven. It was against this cheap answer that Ivan Karamazov protested with unanswerable logic.

Suffering, however, seldom leaves men with so clear a vision as that of Ivan. The morally healthy accusation against God for evil and suffering is turned round into an accusation against man. It is man who is the sinner. It is man who needs forgiveness. It is man who must be justified. The question of God's justice is pushed to one side so that we may occupy ourselves with the question of man's sin. And thus is divine sanction given to my hatred of me which in fact is simply the result of my attempt to cope with my pain, with what hurts. In such circumstances religious belief is a destructive force. It allies itself with the destroyer of mankind. It is Satan masquerading as an angel of light.

It was pointed out at the beginning of the chapter that one of the cruellest things about suffering is its power to isolate the sufferer. But here at least we Christian men who know we are guilty, who know that if mankind suffers it is mankind's own fault, corporately if not individually, who take the side of suffering in its destructive work and claim that it is God's side too, here in this matter of isolation at least we Christian men have looked for consolation. And we have found it by universalizing suffering, by regarding it as ultimate reality itself. For that is how we have used Jesus of Nazareth. That is the purpose to which down the centuries we have put him. Jesus suffered. It is true that he is held to have suffered not for man's innocence, not as a fellow victim of the tragedy which engulfs us all, but for man's sin, for man's culpable wickedness, so that looking at Jesus upon the cross we may hate ourselves all the more and reaffirm our alliance with the pain which torments and destroys us. We have exalted suffering into an attribute of God himself[7] so that suffering thus ceases to be an outrage or even a problem. The point has been put with devastating clarity by Camus: 'In that Christ suffered, and had suffered voluntarily, suffering was no longer unjust and all pain was necessary. In one sense, Christianity's bitter intuition and legitimate pessimism concerning human behaviour is based on

[7] I am of course aware that Patripassianism was technically a heresy.

the assumption that over-all injustice is as satisfying to man as total justice. Only the sacrifice of an innocent god could justify the endless and universal torture of innocence. Only the most abject suffering by God could assuage man's agony. If everything, without exception, in heaven and earth is doomed to pain and suffering, then a strange form of happiness is possible.'[8]

It is not being claimed that Christianity stands or falls with this view, but only that it falls. If it stands, it is upon other foundations which it is our purpose soon to investigate. But Christianity is often in practice confused with the view we have described. And the confusion is illuminating. For it shows what happens when we try to exorcize the brutality of hard facts by fabricating explanations for them. Superficially, the explanations reassure us by appearing to give some sort of rational meaning to a state of affairs which is felt to be irrational and outrageous. But on a deeper level, the appeal of the explanations lies elsewhere. They have been taken on and accepted because they secretly minister to destructive forces within us of which we are largely unaware. In this case our suffering makes us want to hate ourselves. And it is precisely this hatred which our explanations of suffering justify and feed. We suffer because we are guilty. And God suffers because, though innocent, he has voluntarily chosen to hate himself. That is the inner secret logic of God himself becoming in Christ the focus of his own wrath against sin. Because everybody is punished, everybody can be happy – in a way.

Unfortunately, or rather fortunately, the emotional mechanics of this sort of attitude are by now too well investigated and understood to be taken as anything more than psychopathology. The trick has been seen through. Such an attitude is now recognized as the product of human sickness. 'Because the contemplation of Christ's suffering deepens the conviction of man's unworthiness, the old masochistic surrender is allowed to repeat itself in a more refined, not to say sophisticated, manner. We would contend that the fundamental religious motorics of Christianity cannot be understood if one does not understand this and that, furthermore,

[8] Albert Camus, *The Rebel*, translated by Anthony Bower, Hamish Hamilton, 1953, p. 34.

the plausibility of Christianity (at least in its major orthodox forms) stands or falls with the plausibility of this theodicy.'[9]

Well, maybe. But the threat of collapse to established religion is not new. It is as old at least as St John's gospel – 'Destroy this temple and in three days I will raise it up.' Maybe that Christianity as an explanatory system, as a theodicy, will soon collapse because as an explanatory system it always contained within itself the seeds of its own corruption. But if this is now becoming evident, that does not mean that one fraction of the experienced truth and power of resurrection is being taken away from us. On the contrary, the heralded collapse may be precisely the death which is always the necessary prelude to resurrection.

4

Let us therefore abandon comprehensive explanatory systems, theodicies, all the dogma and all the weight, in order to examine at first hand our own experience of suffering.

One fact becomes immediately apparent. The only suffering of which we can be fully or ultimately aware is our own. It is true that by imaginative sympathy we can to some extent understand what other people are feeling, or more accurately, we can to some extent feel what they are feeling. Writers of genius, as we have seen, can do this. But they can do it only because at the time of writing they have identified themselves with the particular individual they are describing, so that, as they write, they themselves *are* John Smith who suffers in this particular way. It is therefore their own experience of suffering they are describing when they describe John Smith. Without genius of this kind, all we are generally capable of understanding is an experience of suffering in others which is identical with or similar to an experience of our own in the past. We feel or live their suffering by refeeling or reliving our own. If somebody suffers in a way in which we have never suffered, we may indeed know that they are suffering, but we shall be unable to feel with them because what they are feeling is to us a closed book. A priest, for instance, if nobody he loves has died prematurely, feels helpless in the presence of suffering of that

[9] P. L. Berger, *The Social Reality of Religion*, Faber & Faber, 1969, p. 78.

kind. If he is sensitive he will be silent because he simply has no way of knowing what the bereaved are going through.

One of the reasons why we can be aware only of our own suffering is that suffering takes place not abstractly in a void, but in terms of a particular life-history with its infinite many-sidedness. Without knowing this infinite many-sidedness from the inside, we cannot tell how the suffering concerned articulates itself with regard to the particular person. Tom, Dick, and Harry may each have been blinded in an accident. But the way in which they feel the cruelty of this misfortune will be different in each case because each is a different person. When we abstract suffering from the person who suffers as though it were an entity on its own, we get a completely false idea of what the suffering entails. We tend to think that the person is *only* his suffering, and this may lead us to get the horror of it, real though it is, out of all proportion. The horror of civilian bombing, for instance, when we read about it in the newspapers during the Spanish Civil War, seemed very much worse than we discovered it in fact was when we in London were bombed, though that was no tea-party. On the other hand, for the callous, abstracting the suffering from its situation in life has the opposite effect. A callous man can think that it is not too bad really for people to be hungry, because he does not himself know what it feels like to be hungry with no hope of a meal in any foreseeable future. *Mutatis mutandis* this is the impression sometimes given by the professionally religious in their expositions of their religion.

If the only suffering of which we can be fully or ultimately aware is our own, then it is obviously useless to have any general theory about suffering, let alone any universal explanations. We may want answers to our metaphysical questions about the why and wherefore, but when given they do not help since they are bogus answers disguising the fact that there are no answers. Explanation of this kind is always in the language of the third party and the onlooker and is concerned with generalities, while our suffering is individual, personal, immediate, and is concerned with me being me and not with things in general being what they are.

5

Suffering is experienced as a threat to what I am. It threatens to diminish and in the end to destroy my personal identity. It forces me to be less and less the person I once knew and felt myself to be until I cease to be that person at all. Resurrection in this context means turning the threat into a promise, so that what would otherwise destroy me becomes the very means by which I am created. In resurrection the suffering which bids fair to diminish and exterminate my personal identity is used on the contrary to enlarge and enrich it. Instead of becoming less myself by suffering, I become more myself. Instead of ceasing to live because of what I suffer, I live more fully and deeply because of it. And this is not a case of suffering in the present leading to fulfilment later, of the hero having made his excursion into suffering and having returned again to happiness in the end. The suffering remains as the medium and agent of the fulfilment and the happiness. This is symbolized in the story of Christ still bearing the marks of the nails and the spear after his resurrection. He has not lost his wounds nor is he glorious in spite of them. His wounds are still there and he is glorious in virtue of them. 'The joy of Easter,' said Simone Weil, 'is not that which follows upon suffering, freedom after the chains, satiety after hunger, reunion after separation. It is joy which lies beyond suffering and achievement. Suffering and joy are in perfect balance. Suffering is the opposite of joy; but joy is not the opposite of suffering.'[10]

6

This deep truth can perhaps be glimpsed at best by means of symbols provided by the visual arts.

In the Academia di Belle Arte in Florence can be found four sculptures which Michelangelo carved for the tomb of Pope Julius. They look unfinished. 'The figures are emerging from rough stone as though they were tearing themselves out of it

[10] The passage can be found in *First and Last Notebooks*, Oxford University Press, 1970, p. 69.

with tremendous effort and pain, drawing towards an assertion of triumph which yet includes within it the agony of the creative protest.'[11] In allowing us to see the cost of their creation, Michelangelo has revealed the cost of our creation. Those four figures are us as we are being torn out of non-being into being by the hammer-blows of our experience, and we are being created not in spite of the blows but because of them. Yet no more than the rough stone do we know what we are being hit into – what form or pattern of beauty is being revealed by the marks of the chisel. Yet a time may come when we are able to feel that somehow the experience of hammer and chisel was worth it, that the experience has not after all reduced us to a mess of meaningless bits and pieces but has provided us with a value and richness we should otherwise have lacked, so that our suffering is now seen to be woven into our joy as an essential part of it.

The same glimpse of resurrection can be seen in the portrait of an old woman by a contemporary painter of genius.[12] The old woman's face is deeply lined as though it had been ploughed up again and again by agony upon agony. It is the face of somebody whom life has tortured without mercy. The furrows speak of wounds and deeper wounds, of sufferings and cares piled one on top of the other. It is the face of somebody who has found life an experience of continuous betrayal. The old woman looks as if no sorrow has passed her by, as though she could never be surprised again by any kind or degree of pain. Yet in his portrayal of this agonizingly tragic face, the artist has given an over-all impression of triumph. In its very lines and furrows the face gives off an invincible strength. The old woman possesses a wisdom and serenity which nothing can take from her. She is in possession of true and indestructible riches. She has looked on the travail of her soul and is satisfied. She is at peace – the peace which can belong only to those who are fully and deeply alive. What the artist has shown is victory over suffering by its acceptance – not the passive acceptance of hopeless resignation, but the active acceptance of one who has been willing to receive her suffering and absorb it

[11] David Anderson, *The Tragic Protest*, S.C.M. Press, 1969, p. 198.
[12] The portrait is in a private collection.

and thus to make it contribute powerfully to what she is. The portrait shows somebody who has become fully a person by means of those very hammer-blows of experience which might have broken her up completely. Yet the face shows little conscious knowledge of her achievement. Her triumph is too real for her to be aware of it much. She is far beyond the stage of seeking artificial boosts in any narcissistic self-congratulation.

A similar image of resurrection is found in the later paintings of Van Gogh. What from one point of view they portray is the horrific and poisonous power of destructive evil. The brush-strokes open our eyes to the hell and damnation which lie every-where – in a field of growing corn, in the sky, in the chairs and tables of a café, in the wall of a house, in the features of a friend. Yet it is by means of this horror of hell that Van Gogh reveals his supreme affirmation of life. For the destructiveness he pitilessly portrays does not lead to destruction. It is, on the contrary, the medium of a superabundant vitality. From the destructiveness itself has been wrenched the power of superhuman life. The fields of corn, the chairs and tables, the walls, the faces of friends, show not one single trace of defeat or despair. They are aglow with a dark and fierce glory. They reveal a world infinitely more alive than the ordinary world of common experience. Hell and dam-nation have themselves been harnessed by Van Gogh to serve the purposes of his creative vision. He has made of darkness itself the light by which he sees – and enables his viewers to see.

7

The paradox presented here by sculptor and painter was expressed by Sartre in terms of a nation's history when he said of his countrymen – 'We have never been more free than under the German occupation.'[13] The brute fact of tyranny, the denial of all political and public freedom, made men aware to an unusual degree of their chains. And in this full recognition of their lack of freedom, men became aware of their true freedom which consists

[13] Jean-Paul Sartre, *Situations*, 3 (Paris), 1948, p. 11.

in the active acceptance of external reality with all its constraints, so that the constraint itself is made into the very context and milieu in which personal freedom is asserted.

8

In terms of an individual life this paradox of death as resurrection has seldom been more magnificently expressed than by Beethoven.[14] He was only thirty when his deafness began to give him serious trouble, and it got steadily and rapidly worse until he was completely deaf. He did not know when his piano was out of tune, and when playing to friends they noticed that he sometimes struck the keys so lightly that no sound came from the piano at all. When applause burst out at the first performance of his Ninth Symphony, he did not hear it and had to be turned round to the audience. Deafness is obviously the worst possible disability for a musician. Beethoven did not hear any of the music he composed during the last fifteen or eighteen years of his life. He did not hear a bar of his Ninth Symphony, his *Missa Solemnis*, his later quartets. And his deafness, as it always does, cut him off from social life and prevented him from forming any intimate relation, so that, although he wanted to marry and was often deeply in love, he remained perforce a bachelor and had no outlet for his affections. The story of his suffering is told in his own letters. 'You can scarcely imagine,' he wrote when he was thirty-one, 'how lonely and sad my life has been during the past two years. My weak hearing haunted me everywhere, and I ran away from people and was forced to appear like a misanthrope, though that is far from being my character.' In the same year he wrote a testament for his brother which was published six months after his death: 'I am compelled to live an exile. If I approach near to people, a feeling of hot anxiety comes over me lest my condition should be noticed – for so it was during these past six months which I spent in the country. How humiliating it was, when

[14] My material has been taken from W. J. Turner's biography, *Beethoven: the Search for Reality*, Ernest Benn, 1927.

someone standing close to me heard a distant flute, and I heard *nothing*, or a *shepherd singing*, and again I heard nothing.' Beethoven goes on to describe his despair. At one time, he says, he was on the point of suicide. But instead of suicide came the miracle of resurrection.

'You will see me as happy as my lot can be here below. Not unhappy, no. That I could never endure. I will seize fate by the throat. It shall never wholly overcome me. How beautiful life is.' A year later he completed the *Eroica Symphony*. From the appearance of that work a new dimension entered into European music which could never be the same again. The succeeding composers of the century – Wagner, Brahms – built upon the foundations Beethoven had laid. By seizing fate by the throat, Beethoven gave us his Third to his Ninth Symphonies, many of his sonatas, *Fidelio*, his *Missa Solemnis*, and his later quartets. Instead of becoming the victim of his fate, he became its master. He used the filthy trick life had played upon him and the terrible constraints it brought as the opportunity to be himself supremely, and in his music to give himself supremely. He transformed his complete deafness into an elected silence which sang to him. And his music bears the marks of the ordeal in which he was perpetually engaged and perpetually the victor. Affirmation is invariably succeeded by a question mark. And the question mark is not quickly disposed of. It returns again and again in a work until it is caught up and resolved in a final synthesis of triumph. 'In *Egmont*, in *Coriolanus*, in the Third, Fifth, Seventh, Ninth, and even the Eighth Symphony you find Beethoven at the very moments of his most delirious, most ecstatic exultation, in his triumphant strength, suddenly interrupting himself with a question. It is as if the voice of an inner censor had spoken and pulled him up. He hesitates, the dominating will reasserts itself and presses forward to a higher peak of triumph. Again the censor speaks and the will, under criticism, struggles intensely to purify itself and rise again. Once more the censor speaks. The will shudders, sheds still more of its dross and lifts what remains of itself with an effort that is anguish to the listeners, and ascends still further. Again the censor speaks. . . . This struggle becomes so frightful in Beethoven's last works –

due to his power of both self-forgetfulness and self-recovery – that we are not always fit to listen to them.'[15]

It is interesting that Beethoven took with him wherever he lived a saying found in an Egyptian temple which he had written out and framed – 'I am that which is.' His suffering challenged him to discover more of himself than that superficial surface of what we are which we often equate with our total selves. The Egyptian text reminds us of the Buddhist injunction – 'Look within; thou *art* Buddha.' Or we could say that, like St Paul, Beethoven found his full and final identity in the eternal creative Word. And from that discovery he arose from the death fate brought him to the glory of his creative triumph.

9

What Beethoven is to Germany, Shakespeare is to England – our supreme genius. It is not, therefore, unexpected that the reality of death and resurrection should proclaim itself in many of his plays. And what we find is not the superficial notion that we pass through and beyond suffering to happiness. The suffering is the raw material of the happiness. The achievement is wrenched out of the despair. Suffering, despair, doubt, evil, are received and assimilated and thus are transposed into another key where they are experienced as fulfilment and joy. It is, as always, the wound-prints themselves which are raised in glory. Shakespeare 'labours to master and assimilate that unassuaged bitterness and sense of rejection so normal a lot to humanity (hence the popularity of *Hamlet*) by drawing the hostile elements within his own world of artistic creation; and this he does mainly through tragedy and its thunderous music; and by seeing that, in spite of logic, his creation is good. By destroying his protagonists, he renders them death-less; by expressing evil, in others and in himself, he renders it innocent.' His is 'a tumult of creative activity, turning every grief into a star, making of his very loathing something "rich and strange".'[16]

The Winter's Tale may here be taken as a model. Leontes, King

[15] Turner, op. cit., pp. 263–4.
[16] G. Wilson Knight, *The Crown of Life*, Methuen, 1965, p. 222.

of Sicily, is baselessly and pathologically jealous of his wife Hermione whom he falsely imagines unfaithful. He becomes the prisoner of his own unmotivated suspicions. Although the Delphic oracle declares Hermione innocent, Leontes disregards it and puts her in prison where later, he learns, she dies. In fact it is a misreport and Hermione continues to live. Thinking her dead and lost, Leontes grieves bitterly for her. His jealousy killed her. But, in the end, she is revealed to him in the speaking likeness of a statue which is really her living self. Leontes greets her with joy as one returned from the dead.

Shakespeare shows us Leontes as the victim of death-dealing suspicions which lead him to deal death to others. He imprisons and 'kills' his wife. He tries to poison her alleged lover. The daughter born to her (and him) in prison he orders to be left on a desert shore to perish (though she is rescued by a shepherd). Leontes' jealousy robs him of everything he loves. It reduces him and all about him to sterility and death. 'Time is throughout present as a backward-flowing thing, swallowing and engulfing; we are sunk deep in the consciousness of dead facts, causes, death.' Yet in the bitterness of his soul, Leontes is purified. He comes to see his suspicions as baseless, and in deepest anguish he mourns for the wife he killed. Over against consciousness of death, there now stands 'the creative consciousness, existing not in time-past but in time-future, and with a sense of causation not behind but ahead, the ever-flowing in of the new and unconditioned, from future to present: this is the consciousness of freedom, in which "every wink of an eye some new grace is born"'. So, first as a statue and then as her living breathing self, Hermione is restored to Leontes. The dead past itself becomes the living present, and is thus raised from the grave. But because Leontes is first confronted by Hermione as a statue, this resurrection is shown 'as no easy release, but rather as a gradual revelation, under terrific dramatic pressure and fraught with excitement with which the watcher's "I" is, by most careful technique, forced into a close subjective identity, so that the immortality revealed is less concept than experience. Nor is it just a reversal of tragedy; rather tragedy is contained, assimilated, transmuted; every phrase of the resurrection scene is soaked in tragic feeling, and the accompanying joy less an antithesis to sorrow as its final flowering. The depths of the "I", which are tragic, are being integrated with the objective delight which is nature's joy.' Man's true estate is shown in terms of creation and miracle. 'The response is a reverential wonder at knowledge of Life where Death was throned.'[17]

Again and again Shakespeare shows us death, either literal or in its various representations – banishment, exile, separation – as the place where life calls men into fullness of living and truth. Leontes' falling truly in love with the 'dead' wife he has wronged only when she is transformed into a statue stands symbolically for all. In the midst of death we are in life – that is Shakespeare's continuous witness to the fact of resurrection, not as concept but as experience.

10

c,   g by means of its very death-dealing qualities can be life-giv.   that is because in our suffering the Eternal Word is made flesh, and that silent presence never ceases to create us in the moment where the First Day and the Last Day are one and the same. As dying and behold we live, as having nothing and yet possessing all things, that is life eternal here now.

11

But what men of genius reveal to us in their art may, from one point of view, seem unattainable by us ordinary mortals. The vision given by genius is at the time compelling in its truth and power. But it may be rather like those strips of magnesium which used to be lit at children's parties as an indoor firework – the super-brilliant light lasts only a few seconds leaving the room looking even dimmer than before. To what is shown us by a Michelangelo, a Beethoven, a Shakespeare, we may respond with a total unqualified Yes. But what happens when we get home? Usually we retain the negative side of their vision. We know the

[17] Ibid., pp. 126–7.

constraint and suffering they reveal, the forms of despair and deadness they worked on as their raw material. What eludes us is their triumph. In the gallery or at the performance we saw the possibility of triumph as in a lightning flash. But once we are home it becomes no more than a theoretical possibility, and once in the realm of theory we can use logic to defeat ourselves. We reason that as we cannot transform our suffering into sculpture or music or poetry, how on earth is it possible for us to take fate by the throat? How can our commonplace selves make our destructive suffering creative? How can folk like us find the well of life in the arid deserts of our own death?

Perhaps, therefore, we should try in terms of our own ordinary existence to work out what genius reveals. Seeing we are not a Beethoven or a Shakespeare, how in our suffering are we raised from the dead?

The superficial answer to suffering is the attempt to escape from it as much and as best we can, to ignore it as far as possible distracted from distraction by distraction. So we overwork or pursue pleasure relentlessly, clutching at either of them like a drowning man clutching at a straw. Or we tense ourselves up in some way or other, building around us a brick wall whose primary purpose is to protect us from ourselves but which also inevitably cuts us off from others. But this attempt to escape from suffering by distraction or isolation does not work. The power of suffering as death-dealing is not so easily evaded. We may to some extent be able from time to time to forget what is gnawing at us, but the gnawing continues, the destructive force goes on slowly killing us. Our identity is diminished, however successfully we may make ourselves unconscious of the fact for shorter or longer periods. And our oblivion is a double one. For in attempting to escape our destructive suffering we have also made ourselves blind to its potentially creative power. We have run away from our fate instead of becoming its master.

In the biblical legend Jacob wrestles all night with the mysterious stranger who has attacked him and is bent on killing him. At dawn the stranger tries to leave. And Jacob says – 'I will not let thee go unless thou bless me.' So the potential destroyer blesses

Jacob and promises him rich fulfilment, 'for as a prince hast thou power with God and with men, and hast prevailed'.[18]

When, instead of struggling with our assailant we try to escape from him and forget our suffering, then no blessing or promise can be given. In protecting ourselves by attempted forgetfulness from our fate we also insulate ourselves against the means of becoming our full selves.

Here we should make clear that among the various forms of suffering – physical disease, accident, catastrophe – the ultimate form is always mental and emotional. For the objective illness or accident or catastrophe accomplishes its deadly work in what we call our state of mind or our feelings. It is as beings who think and feel that we are vulnerable to the onslaughts of suffering. And in mind and feeling we can suffer just as much, and generally far more, when our suffering is linked to no physical illness or external distress. For when linked to something objective or external our suffering seems to make some sort of sense, however bloody that sense may be. But when our suffering comes only from within our own heart and mind with nothing outside to pin it on, then it seems utterly and senselessly malignant. We suffer we know not why. But of whatever kind it is, suffering attacks us in the very centre of our identity. It is myself as a person who is mauled.

12

But if we do not attempt to run away from our suffering, what then is the alternative?

The alternative is to accept and receive it, to take it on as a part of what we are. For in doing this we discover new and hitherto unknown and unimagined areas of our being. We discover that the self we took as our total self was in fact only a small fraction of what we are, that we have reserves of strength, and insight and courage and heroism and love and compassion of which so far we have been totally unaware. That is how suffering can by acceptance create us – by activating and making accessible to us powers within us which hitherto were dormant and only potential so that

[18] Genesis 32: 26.

we had no inkling of their existence. So when the suffering first comes, ignorant of our dormant potential, we feel simply that we cannot bear it. The suffering, we feel, is too much for us and will destroy us. It seems therefore that we must either resign completely and give way to the destructive power and let the waves drown us, or try to salvage some shreds of identity by means of self-pity or by taking the side of the suffering's assault and thereby obtaining some kind of perverse masochistic satisfaction in our own destruction. But this capitulation to suffering so that it drowns us, or we seek to console ourselves for it by self-pity or masochistic pleasure, this capitulation works itself out in terms of the limited self which is the only self of which so far we are aware. It is that limited self which feels it cannot bear it and must be swept away. Yet when, by miracle, we accept the suffering, receive it, take it on board, then we find that this limited self is an illusion, that we are infinitely more than we ever imagined, so that we can after all take the suffering and in taking it become fuller, deeper, richer people because a dormant potential within us has been roused to activity and life, and we know ourselves to be more than previously we had even a hint of. Thus does the destructive power of suffering become creative and what is death-dealing become life-giving.

But we shall not know that this is going on. There will be nothing like a glorious certainty that we are mastering our fate by assimilating it and by assimilating it growing into fullness. All we shall feel is much pain with spasmodic and very faint glimmers of hope. The faint glimmer of hope will be obscure and undefined. It will be a glimmer of hope for we know not what. Yet for all its being feeble, intermittent, and without content, the hope is the call to us of our own future, indicating that we are not only at an end but also at a beginning. For the hope, weak and unidentified though it is, is a sign that a transformation has begun – the transformation of the death-dealing past into the life-giving future. The hope shows that somewhere within us we are somehow obscurely aware that the suffering we meet and receive will call forth a self capable of digesting it, a self therefore which is greater and fuller than the self at present known to us.

But the price of this transformation and growth is willingness to feel the pain of our suffering, however acute it may be. And the pain will generally seem like one undifferentiated meaningless horror. We shall not be able to distinguish between the pain which belongs to the destruction of the limited self manacled to the past, and the pain which belongs to the birth and creation of a fuller self. (For our birth and creation involve pain – the woman in travail is its inevitable symbol.) But in fact when we receive our suffering and are willing to feel its pain, it is both sorts of pain which are hitting us in the face – the pain of dying and the pain of being born. It hurts when the manacles which chain us to the past are broken. And it hurts when by our experience we are opened up almost forcibly to the future. It seems like one single hurt, leaving us all too agonizingly aware of its destructive power and almost totally unaware of its creative power, save for the faint glimmer of undefined hope.

Yet that hope is like a grain of mustard seed which when it is sown is the least of all the seeds, but grows up into the greatest of all plants so that the fowls of the air lodge under the shadow of it. For that first faint intermittent glimmer of hope is the impact upon us of the Eternal Word calling us into our future, calling us into being, so that we grow and become people who can support others in their distress and give them shade now and again from the fierce heat of their own suffering.

13

When considering what within us is so far only potential and dormant, we must take note of the obvious fact that it includes not only what we should call good and creative but also much that we should call evil and destructive. And a great deal of suffering – perhaps a universal form of it – consists in our being savagely confronted by what within us is evil and destructive: the utterly ruthless self-assertion which attempts to impose its will regardless of the cost to others and the many by-products of this murderous aggression – cruelty, callousness, possessiveness, jealousy, envy, hatred, malice. In this context the attempt to run away from our suffering takes the form of disguising these destructive forces within ourselves and pretending for our own benefit that they do not exist and that we are really, when it comes down to it, nice, kind, benevolent people. And it is true, we are nice, kind, and benevolent. But at the same time we are also the opposite. And a great deal of our energy is spent in keeping the negative destructive forces out of sight and out of mind. When goodness is equated with this sort of escapism and evasion it appears anaemic and castrated, and we are harbouring dangerous enemies unawares.

The ultimate challenge of life is squarely to face our capacity for evil and destruction and by receiving and assimilating it to transform it into what is positive and creative, so that the dynamic of our evil potential becomes harnessed to what within us is constructive and good. This acceptance and transformation of our own destructiveness is the *sine qua non* of all personal growth, and it means that in some form or other the bloody sweat of Gethsemane is the universal human vocation which must be undergone by everybody who chooses life instead of death. When therefore we are tormented by rage and jealousy and hatred and envy, together with the stifling frustration and despair in which they issue, it is not, as we generally imagine, a sign that things have gone radically wrong. On the contrary, it indicates that we are indeed taking fate by the throat, grappling with our endless death-dealing past, facing ourselves as the products of causes which go back to the dawn of time, refusing any longer to keep them locked up out of sight, but wrestling with them as Jacob wrestled with the stranger, compelling them to leave a blessing behind where it looked as if there was only a curse. For these evil destructive things are evil and destructive only in so far as we attempt to exclude them from what we are and keep them at arm's length from ourselves. When we admit them into awareness, although at first they appear to reek havoc with us and produce all but intolerable turmoil and distress, they are in fact being taken up into our constructive creative selves and contribute as nothing else can to our power for good.

Jesus told us to love our enemies, for by loving them we may turn them into our friends. This applies supremely to the enemy within. For our own worst enemy is always ourselves. And if with patience and compassion I can love that murderous man, that cruel callous man, that possessive envious jealous man, that malicious man who hates his fellows, that man who is me, then I am on the way to converting him into everything which is dynamically good and lovely and generous and kind and, above all, superabundantly alive with a life which is contagious. That is the goal to which we are being led by means of our agony and bloody sweat, our cross and passion – to our glorious resurrection whereby vitality and strength and joy are brought to others in what is truly a coming of the Holy Ghost. For by a strange transmutation the enemy of mankind within ourselves is discovered as nothing other than the Eternal Word creating us – that Word whose characteristic manifestation is invariably in the form of a figure whose wounds are his glory and whose death is his resurrection.

When through love of what I am I accept myself as a potential murderer, then I find myself capable of murdering ignorance, prejudice, suspicion, and fear. When I accept myself as possessive, jealous, and envious, I find that what I covet earnestly are the best gifts of which the greatest is the charity which is willing to suffer and strive for the fulfilment of others. When I accept myself as hating and malicious, I find that what I hate and abhor is everything which corrupts and destroys that tender love for the men and women I know intimately, whose presence, whose very existence, is my supreme happiness and satisfaction. It is this conversion and transformation of evil into good, of destruction into creation, going on within us now as we wrestle with our fate, which is summed up and represented in the figure of the Eternal Word crucified and raised from the dead. For it is not a case of asking – 'Who can go up to heaven? (that is to bring Christ down) or, Who can go down to the abyss? (that is to bring Christ up from the dead).'[19] For the Word is near us now in our hearts, and it is in our hearts now in the present that the Word is made flesh, suffers, dies, and is raised from the dead. That ultimate miracle is

[19] Romans 10:7.

a daily and hourly occurrence as common, and from one point of view as ordinary, as mankind itself.

William James said that the fundamental keynote of his experience was always reconciliation, and his words are worth quoting as they describe with his characteristic lucidity what I have been attempting to describe: 'It is as if the opposites of the world, whose contradictoriness and conflict make all our difficulties and troubles, were melted into unity. Not only do they, as contrasted species, belong to one and the same genus, *but one of the species*, the nobler and better one, *is itself the genus and so soaks up and absorbs its opposite into itself.* This is a dark saying, I know, when thus expressed in terms of common logic, but I cannot wholly escape from its authority.'[20]

14

About our fate there is always something external. It often confronts us as outward circumstance. It always confronts us as inner disposition. But in both cases it is external in the sense that it is willed upon us without our choice by forces over which we have no control – the forces of heredity and environment by which we are caught up in the mechanistic law of cause and effect. Our freedom consists in our consciously choosing what has thus already been chosen for us. It is in this way that we internalize our fate so that it becomes part and parcel of what we are instead of standing threateningly over against us.

The fate of Jesus, for example, was external to him. He was caught up as a victim in a net of political and religious forces beyond his control. He was the victim too of his own implacable temperament which made him enemies and led one of his friends to betray him. He was really and truly at the mercy of his fate. He had no magical abracadabra in reserve by which he could put everything all right and himself on top. Yet he voluntarily chose the fate he could not escape, and thus changed the necessity thrust upon him into the means of freely fulfilling his personal vocation, so that he could say with truth – 'No man taketh my life from me,

[20] William James, *The Varieties of Religious Experience*, Longmans, Green, 1952, p. 379 (his italics).

but I lay it down of myself. I have power to lay it down, and I have power to take it again.'[21] And similarly, like Jesus, can men find their freedom in what otherwise compels them, in response to that Eternal Word which is continuously calling us into being.

It is by being accepted, assimilated, absorbed, and consciously willed that the iron decrees of fate can be overcome, not in the sense of being eliminated, but in the sense of being made to contribute to what we freely are and to what we freely purpose. 'Ours is a being whose concrete essence is to be in every way *involved* and therefore to find itself at grips with a fate which it must not only undergo, but also make its own by somehow re-creating it from within.'[22]

The alternative is to be destroyed –

> . . . for pride it is
> To think you can be stronger than the Gods

– and defy head-on or by blind unawareness what they have decreed. That way only nemesis lies.

As Vishnu says to Arjuna who is tempted to run away from his fate: 'Fixing thy thoughts on Me, thou shalt surmount all difficulties by My grace. But if, prompted by thine own ego, thou wilt not hearken, thou shalt perish. Shouldst thou, relying on thy ego, think, "I will not fight", thy effort is in vain, for Nature will compel thee. Bound by thine own deeds which are born of thine own nature, thou wilt do what, in thy delusion, thou wouldest not, for thou art without mastery.'

Or in the words of a twentieth-century prophet – 'Only the man who is able *consciously* to affirm the power of the vocation confronting him becomes a personality; he who succumbs to it falls a prey to the blind flux of happening and is destroyed. The greatness and liberating effect of all genuine personality consists in this, that it subjects itself of free choice to its vocation and consciously translates into its own individual reality what would lead only to ruin if it were lived unconsciously.'[23]

[21] John 10:18.

[22] Gabriel Marcel, *Being and Having*, Dacre Press, 1949, p. 116 (his italics).

[23] C. G. Jung, *The Integration of Personality*, Kegan Paul, 1940, p. 296 (his italics).

Dante has stated the matter at its simplest – 'In his will is our peace', only the phrase has become trivialized by a shallow piety and used in the service of a passive resignation which is totally sterile. In fact Dante is here saying much the same thing as Nietzsche in *The Twilight of the Idols* when he speaks of 'the affirmation of life even in its most familiar and severe problems . . . to realize in fact the eternal delight of becoming, that delight which ever involves in itself the joy of assimilating'.[24]

15

Suffering thus assimilated is suffering in its very destructiveness transformed into what creates us. Even when the suffering is due to objective outward circumstance, like physical illness or catastrophe, it mauls, as we have seen, the centre of our personal identity so that we suffer mentally and spiritually. The pain is in our heart and mind. But what otherwise would destroy us, if by miracle it is received and absorbed, leads us to discover that the self is not set within the narrow limits we had imagined, but possesses an infinite potential for development and growth, for that eternal delight of becoming, as Nietzsche called it. But to speak of potential and growth is only one way of putting it. For all growth both in the natural and the spiritual world is a continuing miracle of creation, a calling of things that are not into existence. This coming to be is the creative mystery of all life. And resurrection is precisely coming to be. It is a calling of the non-existent into being. It is the giving of life to what has no life. Suffering diminishes life and finally destroys it. But transformed by active acceptance (in itself the fruit of a mysterious giving of life) suffering is instrumental in raising up a new and fuller identity. It is turned into the agent of resurrection. In this sense it is by losing our life that we find it, and it is by dying that we live. Suffering, in itself utterly malevolent and death-dealing, now becomes the blessing by means of which we are raised to

[24] Friedrich Nietzsche, *The Twilight of the Idols*, translated by A. M. Ludovici (vol. 14 of *The Complete Works of Friedrich Nietzsche*, edited by Oscar Levy), J. N. Foulis, 1911, p. 139.

more abundant life. We are reminded yet once again of the print of the nails and of the spear – in the words of Charles Wesley's hymn: 'Those dear tokens of his passion still his dazzling body bears.'

What we have called active acceptance is only another name for love. The mysterious giving of life which enables us to accept our pain is one of the forms in which love is at work. It is not that we love the pain so that we hate the self which the pain is destroying (that is masochism), but that we love ourselves, diminished, maimed, tortured, made ugly by the pain though we are. We love ourselves as the maiden in the legend loved the beast and by her love transformed him into the prince he really was. That love for ourselves whereby our ugliness is made beautiful, our bankruptcy turned into riches and our torture into joy – that love for ourselves flows from the creative love of the Eternal Word which has loved us from all eternity and in which we discover our true identity – who and what we really are. 'Man finds in his heart, "deeper even than sin" (the phrase is St Isaac the Syrian's) the beginning of an ascent in which the universe seems more and more unified.'[25] 'I can be led to recognize that deep down in me there is something other than me, something further within me than I am myself.'[26] And since our pain is the agent of this discovery and ascent, the agent of resurrection, we love our wounds, not for their own destructive selves, but because we see in them the hope and promise of transformation. They are the harbingers of new abundant life. They lead us to a first glimpse of our infinite possibilities, even as they bang upon and break down that limited self which we have so far equated with all we are. We see in our wounds beyond their evil power to a redemption in which they will be not against us but on our side, and contribute positively to our freedom and fullness.

'What is a merciful heart? It is a heart which burns with love for the whole of creation – for men, for birds, for beasts, for demons, for every creature.' That statement by St Isaac the

[25] V. Lossky, *The Mystical Theology of the Eastern Church*, James Clarke, 1957, p. 107.

[26] Marcel, *Being and Having*, p. 124.

Syrian (seventh century) is at its most significant in its inclusion of demons among the objects of love. For in the mythology of his day demons were responsible for all the ills and suffering which befall us, and in exhorting us to love demons St Isaac shows that he believed them capable of and destined for redemption, so that they will contribute to our glory as now they hurt and bruise us.

It is a characteristic insight of Eastern Orthodoxy with its emphasis on transfiguration, by which the God-bearing capacity of all things will be revealed – even of demons. 'In a humble village church in Russia an old peasant woman set a candle before the picture of the Last Judgement. "Why do you do that?" somebody asked. And she answered: "No one seems to be praying for him. We ought to pray for him too." She meant "For the devil", but she would not speak his name in the church. In this simple soul an all-embracing, deep, pure love gave hope for the final blessedness of everyone, and this hope in its turn strengthened and increased her love.'[27]

16

The demand that what distresses us should be recognized, honoured, loved, and thereby assimilated, so that it contributes creatively to what we are, is found among the Nichiren sect of Buddhism in Japan, in their practice of exorcism.[28] The possessed person must be brought to the condition where the possessing entity – usually a discontented dead spirit or witch animal – is compelled to speak through the patient's mouth – to name itself and to state the reason for its malicious attack. Often there is quite a long dialogue between the exorcist and the spirit in which all the circumstances of the attack are elicited. Finally the exorcist asks what the spirit *wants* in order to leave the sufferer. In nearly every case the answer is 'a little shrine set up to it and an offering made to it every day'. If this is done it promises to turn over a new leaf and *protect* the patient rather than molest him. When the exorcist undertakes to see that this is done, the

[27] Stefan Zankov, *The Eastern Orthodox Church*, S.C.M. Press, 1929, p. 65.
[28] I owe this information to Miss C. E. Blacker, Lecturer in Japanese in the University of Cambridge.

patient sometimes falls flat on the floor. When a little later he recovers, he is usually free of the possession.

Here we see the main features of the pattern we have been considering – the external necessity, its recognition and confrontation, its absorption and assimilation by giving it a permanent shrine in the house and paying it loving honour, and its positive contribution to the person it formerly set out to destroy; it will now protect him.

To find our freedom in the fulfilment of our vocation, and to find our vocation in the inescapable fate put upon us by necessity, and thus to find a self which extends infinitely in the literal sense (for it finds its identity in the Eternal Word) beyond the range of that confined cabined self which we imagined was all we were – that, in summary, is the experience of suffering and resurrection.

17

It may at this point be objected that salvation has here been considered in too individualistic terms.

In so far as this is a theoretical objection it can be disregarded. We must speak what we feel not what we ought to say, even if it is in terms of what we ought to say that we are generally criticized (for theory is cheap enough). Yet this objection need not be theoretical. Our sense of belonging to our world, and especially to one another, is real and goes deep. We feel our interconnection with our fellow men too strongly for it not to enter into our experience of resurrection. If by assimilating our suffering we make it minister to the building up of our personal identity, if in this sense we are raised from the dead, how does the power of this miracle impinge upon others?

In the first place it does so in a very obvious way, as we can see from the people we meet. They can be divided into two – those who drain us of vitality, and those who make us feel more alive. This distinction is of course a complex one. It includes such matters as age, background, the presence or absence of common interests, the presence or absence of sex appeal, and so on. But when these many factors have been taken into account, it remains true that the bloodsuckers are those who are running away from their fate, who are too frightened to accept the necessity laid upon them and who therefore, instead of assimilating their suffering and taking it on board, either remain closed up tightly against it and so against life as a whole, or who allow suffering to swamp them so that they give off perpetual self-pity. The closed-up irritate us by boring us since they are too shut in to give us anything. The swamped irritate us by making us feel guilty since we imagine we are luckier than they are and this seems unfair. The people, on the other hand, who make us feel more alive are those who have taken their own load upon their shoulders and have found that it lifts them up rather than drags them down. They are open to life since they have looked fear in the face and in their agony have laughed at it, and therefore they have everything to give. By their mere presence they radiate a courage to be and the courage is contagious. They make us glad to be alive.

We have here described these two types of people in their ideal pure form. In practice each of us is a mixture of both, with one or the other predominating perhaps steadily or perhaps from time to time. But in so far as we have found resurrection in our suffering, to that extent we shall enliven and encourage others, not of course by preaching at them or taking measures for their good, but simply by being what we are.

As thus we cannot keep our resurrection to ourselves, our salvation cannot be individualistic. In so far as we are ourselves being saved, to that extent we shall inevitably be helping to save others.

When suffering forces us to break through the illusory barriers of the closed-up ego and we discover a selfhood which is no longer limited but caught up in the identity of the Eternal Word, then we no longer regard self as a possession which must be clutched at and guarded at all costs. That is the ultimate meaning of poverty. When we regard self as some limited entity which we possess and must guard, then what we possess in fact possesses us. We are not free to do what we like, for we must for ever be concerned with protecting our property. We say of a house-proud woman that she is the prisoner of the house she looks after, that she is possessed by the house she possesses. So are we possessed by the self we consider ourselves to possess. It hinders us from being what we are and so from giving ourselves. We are its prisoners like the house-proud woman. In these circumstances what suffering does is to destroy the house so that we have to find our home in the limitless spaces of the world. And in doing so, we discover our freedom. We can now give ourselves fully without inhibition because we know that the self is not some limited entity we possess. We no longer confuse having with being. To have is to be limited by what we have, so that if we have twenty and give away four we are left with only sixteen. But to be is to partake of infinity. We are because the Eternal Word is. And however much of ourselves we give away, it is still true of us that we are, and that we are in the same sense and to the same degree.

When therefore suffering reduces us to absolute poverty and we *have* nothing more to give because the limited self we once imagined ourselves to possess has been blown to smithereens, that is the point where we can begin to *be*, and can give ourselves totally because we have no more fear of losing anything. Hence the paradox we have often repeated of our having nothing and yet possessing all things, of our dying and behold we live, of our being poor yet making many rich.

It is only when we know that we do not possess the self and are therefore poor in this final sense, it is only when thus we cease to *have* and begin to *be*, that we can give. Suffering and resurrection are therefore the very quintessence of charity. Far from being limited to anything individualistic, in so far as we are raised up from our suffering we are to that extent available to the world.

18

But there is a less obvious but no less important way in which our resurrection is not for ourselves alone but for others.

The acceptance of our suffering involves, as we have seen, the acceptance of dark destructive forces within the depths of our being – the murderous aggression, the jealousy as cruel as the grave, the malice, and so forth. To become aware of the enemy of mankind within us as part and parcel of what we are involves the acutest pain. By becoming aware of our own evil we can, as we saw, absorb it into the positive constructive side of our nature so that the evil is transformed into good.

This recognition, absorption, and transformation of our own evil has effects far beyond our individual selves. For we are inextricably bound up with one another, and what happens to us individually has its repercussions within the whole group among which we live. When we become aware of our own evil we become aware of an evil at work among the group – destructively at work because in the group it is unrecognized, and being unrecognized it cannot be absorbed. By our recognition of our own evil and our absorption of it, we are absorbing an evil which is communal. And the extent of our recognition and absorption is the extent to which we are accomplishing something for the group as a whole. When, therefore, we feel the terrifying strength of our own drives to aggression and destruction, when we are tortured by jealousy and are confronted by the stark frustration of our malice, and when this leads us to deadness and despair, although we feel completely shut in within our own damned selves, we are in fact accomplishing something of inestimable value for the community as a whole. For the evil which is at work unbeknown in the community, the evil which is driving the community but of which the community is unconscious, has come to consciousness in us, and our recognition and absorption of it helps to liberate the community from the evil spell of which it is unknowingly the victim. 'An individual's shadow [i.e. his evil side] is invariably bound up with the collective shadow of his group, and as he digests his own evil, a fragment of the collective evil is invariably co-digested at the same time. . . . The individual assumes personal responsibility for part of the burden of the collective, and he decontaminates this evil by integrating it into his own inner processes of transformation. If the operation is successful, it leads to an inner liberation of the collective, which in part at least is redeemed from this evil.'[29]

[29] Eric Neumann, *Depth Psychology and a New Ethic*, Hodder & Stoughton, 1969, p. 130.

Thus do our suffering and resurrection avail for others. The figure of Christ in Gethsemane feeling the sin of the world as his own, and thereby taking it away, is representative of us all. We share in that liberating work of sin-bearing when at the cost of maybe untold mental suffering we become aware of the destructive horror and confusion within us. For the horror and confusion are mankind's. And when in us some part of them has come into awareness and been transformed by being integrated constructively with what we are, then to that extent we have helped forward the redemption of mankind. In resurrection our own personal suffering is vicarious. But each man can discover this only for himself by means of his own individual suffering. He cannot make any general theory out of his own private experience. For what has been true of him may not be true of the next man.

19

We are left with the familiar problem we have throughout been unable to answer: why one person is taken and the other left, why suffering raises one man from the dead while it destroys another, why the miracle has come to Tom while it passes Dick by. We do not know. The most we can do is to pretend to know.

But if, however vaguely and faintly, our hearts are even slightly stirred by the hope of resurrection now, it is a sign that the miracle is upon us.

CHAPTER SIX

RESURRECTION & DEATH

So far our concern has been with those death-dealing properties of human life which are the occasions in the present of our resurrection. The deadness of the body as a slave-machine can be raised up to the glory of its own life. The final frustration of the mind as no more than an observing and calculating instrument can lead it to receive its capacity for communion with what it surveys, and thus to come into life-giving riches. The past, in so far as it squeezes the life out of us by imposing upon us its accumulated necessities, can be transformed by the freedom of a goodness which is creative and which therefore actually changes the situation. And the sheer destructiveness of suffering, by being taken on by the person and assimilated, can be the means whereby we pass beyond that strait-jacket of a self which is all we have been aware of so far, to the discovery of a self which is unlimited because it finds its identity in the Eternal Word. In these various ways we can come to a knowledge of life where death was throned and experience resurrection as a present reality.

We are left, however, with the brute fact of physical death and its antecedents. However much people may triumph in the ways we have described, they grow old, their powers fail, mentally and spiritually no less than physically, until in the end they are reduced in the literal sense to the dust of death. What does all the talk of resurrection amount to if it leads finally and inevitably to the grave? What are these miracles of resurrection worth if in the end we are to be destroyed after all? And even worse than the prospect of our own destruction in death is the much bitterer fact that those we loved may have already died. Perhaps while they were alive they did indeed find resurrection in life's death-dealing qualities. But what of it, if now they are literally dead and buried?

No discussion of resurrection can evade the issue of physical death. For it is precisely in physical death that life's destructive forces reach their climax and appear to win their final victory.

2

An easy course here is to take over a theoretical orthodoxy (as though theoretical affirmation in itself could solve anything). There is the orthodoxy of what often calls itself scientific humanism which affirms that physical death is the final end. And there is the orthodoxy of the Christian churches which affirms that physical death is only the prelude to our being raised up to an endless life of perfect fulfilment. When we take over one or other of these orthodoxies *tout court*, we are being driven to a large extent by unconscious factors of which it would be well for us to become aware.

If we are pessimists, if in unknown ways we hate life and have a grudge against it, or if temperamentally we find suspense intolerable and wish therefore to have everything cut and dried, it will encourage us to affirm that death is the final end. And we shall not fail to find reasonable arguments for the conclusion we have already at least half chosen. If, on the other hand, we are optimists, if we invariably shut our eyes to life's negative and destructive forces and organize ourselves against seeing them, if, in face of all evidence to the contrary, we insist that life is rose-coloured, then it will help us to opt for the orthodoxy which affirms that death is only the entrance to fullness of life.

Yet in face of the extremity of death curious reversals will take place. The congenital pessimist may be driven to optimism by the sheer pressure of his need and insist that there must be a heaven, just as the man dying of thirst in the desert will insist that an oasis *must* be in view. Or the congenital optimist may be so shaken by the destructive reality which in the death of a loved one has at last forced itself on his attention that his defences are completely broken, despair surges in like a flood-tide, and he insists that beyond death there is and can be nothing.

Orthodoxies, whether they affirm the future life or deny it, should be treated with the utmost caution. For when taken over uncritically they are little more than the repository of our own projected fantasies, many of them unconscious. What would serve us best here is evidence. But in the nature of the case there can be no evidence, for death remains the undiscovered country from whose bourn no traveller returns. It is true that psychical research supplies evidence to a certain degree, but it is of extremely limited significance. All that can reasonably be inferred from the evidence so far available is that 'certain people survive death for a certain period of time'.[1] And this is not evidence for immortality, let alone immortality on a general scale.

In the absence of anything like adequate evidence from the dead themselves, if we are not to be taken in by our own wishes and subjective fantasies, we must rely on our own experience in this present life – experience of the kind we have discussed in the previous chapters – to give us some reasonably firm ground for our views concerning what happens when we die. We shall therefore select various features of our discussion so far of resurrection to discover the relevance they may have to the question of the future life: whether physical death is the final end or the gateway to another life. We shall here call in evidence nothing which cannot and has not been experienced by ordinary people in the world.

3

We have seen that the mind is not only a machine for observing the empirical world and making calculations about it, and that there are other valid ways of knowing besides that used by the scientific method. If we limit the act of knowing to this one particular way of knowing, there is a sense in which we shall know nothing whatever deeply. For the mind as an observing and calculating machine breaks up what it observes into the fragments its method requires and then insulates us from the fragments, so that we can know a thing only in its disrupted externality and not in the unity and immediacy of its total identity. If we are to know places, people, and works of art deeply, then we have to open ourselves to them in a more comprehensive way of knowing in

[1] I owe this summary, given me in 1968, to the late Professor C. D. Broad, for many years President of the Psychical Research Society.

which we receive them into ourselves and establish communion with them. But this does not reduce them to sheer subjectivity and render them no more than the product of our own fantasies. On the contrary, objectivity is the *sine qua non* of communion, for the other as objectively itself must be there to establish communion with. And this knowledge as communion is identical with love.

If in any full sense I cannot know my home ground or my wife or Velázquez's pictures or Beethoven's music by weighing and measuring them, drawing up an inventory of their particulars, or reducing them to the dimensions of a mathematical model, then the fact that these procedures are completely out of the question with regard to the future life is no proof whatever of its non-existence. The cognitive grounds in terms of which some people deny the possibility of life after death – that such life is not susceptible to scientific investigation – would, if consistently applied, rob life on earth of all its meaning and value. If what science cannot know is not knowledge, then life on earth would be impoverished to the point of virtual bankruptcy. But nobody in fact lives life on these conditions, for our humanity is stronger than our logic.

This, of course, does not in any way prove that there is a future life. But it does show that the claim to disprove it on scientific grounds is crassly superficial in terms of our experience of life here now. As always, in considering both this life and the possibility of the next, we must beware of becoming the victims of the intellect-bound mind. 'Philosophy lives in words, but truth and fact well up into our lives in ways that exceed verbal formulation. There is in the living act of perception always something which glimmers and twinkles and will not be caught and for which reflection comes too late.'[2] For what in the last resort we perceive is not an object we classify but a presence we feel.

[2] William James, *The Varieties of Religious Experience*, Longmans, Green, 1952, p. 446.

4

The prelude to resurrection as we experience it in this life is always powerlessness. We cannot raise ourselves by our own bootstrings. The body, reduced to the condition of a slave-machine, cannot give itself the glory of its own life. All it can do when let off the leash is to run beserk in the pursuit of its unsatisfying compulsions. Or, when off-form, the tennis player or painter was unable to order arm and hand into adequate activity. Or, as members of the various societies to which we find ourselves belonging, we are prisoners of the past, and even more obviously so in the sufferings which come our way. In both we are the predetermined products of the mechanical law of cause and effect. And there is no formula or technique for getting ourselves out of this prison. We are impotently chained to where we are, and in these circumstances our release to freedom and life is on the level of sheer impossibility. It is the defiance of the absurd. Christians find in Christ nailed to the cross the universal symbol of this powerlessness. 'Impossibility leads straight to the heart of passion, the passion of man, the passion of God.'³ Physical death confronts us with impossibility in its most acute and final form. How can there be any future for this person who has ceased to be? How can these dry bones live? But the impossibility we experience when confronted with physical death is not something new. We have already known it in our experience of deadness, despair, powerlessness, suffering, when we have been one wide wound all of us. Yet the impossible occurred. From our helpless state with no prospect of a future we were raised to newness of life in which the future became ours. If in this life we have experienced impossibility as the inevitable background of resurrection, can that experience leave us unaffected when we consider the impossibility which belongs to physical death?

Our experience of resurrection in this life has been the result of miracle. When here and now we have known ourselves raised from the dead, we have in that experience apprehended ourselves

³ Monica Furlong, in the *New Christian*, 15 May 1969, p. 9.

as being somehow created by a power which is beyond us. The mechanical order of cause and effect was broken into by something outside it – a power which for want of a better description we have called the Eternal Word. When, in our story of George and Margaret, George's body was raised to life by his falling in love with Margaret, Margaret was the occasion of the miracle and its sacramental medium. But the new life George found and which energized within him was the result of a creative act whose source could not ultimately be found simply in what either he was or Margaret was. What she triggered off was a process of becoming, a giving of life, which like all life was ultimately mysterious. Or when a man is raised up from his own dead past to a goodness which in terms of that past is uncaused, that is a miracle because his mental and emotional constitution hitherto provided at best inadequate grounds for the goodness now in operation. His goodness thus shows him being created by what is beyond him. And when his goodness raises others from their own dead past, he becomes himself the instrument of a creativity which he does not possess but which rather possesses him. Or when a man is able to assimilate his suffering, and, by voluntarily choosing the necessity of his fate, makes it contribute to his growth as a person so that in consequence he has all the more of himself to give to others, what is that but miracle? It is his being called into being. It is his being created. It is life itself raising him up from the deadening effect of his constriction.

It is easy for us to forget that life consists in receiving. Yet when we examine our human experience we find that the essence of life is its givenness. 'Every wink of an eye some new grace is born.' We are continuously called into being, continuously nourished and nurtured on every level of what we are by the givenness of what we cannot make. Our physical life in its givenness is miracle. Our mental and emotional life is miracle. When in our mind and heart life rises to consciousness and our creative imagination is stirred into activity, whence comes this power to body forth the form of things unknown?

One of the ways in which in this book we have tried to spell out this givenness of life, its unceasing creativity, is to speak of a limited self which is illusory in so far as we equate it with our total self, but which, under the impact of life's creative power, can be seen through for the illusion it is as we come to discover our full selves in the Eternal Word – in what, in other words, must remain always largely unknown. And once we discover and accept the fact that we are what must thus remain largely unknown, and that it is upon this unknown that we depend for everything – for all we are and do – then the miracle of life's givenness becomes inescapably manifest. It becomes undeniably evident that the secret of life consists not in our possessing it but in our continually being given it.

The miracle of our being given life beyond the grave is no greater than the miracle of our continually being given life here. Creativity is ever one and the same. It is always the calling into being of what is non-existent; and to those who are created it means for ever receiving what for ever is being given. If in this life we know that we are poor, that we are nothing and have nothing which we are not receiving from the unknown, then it will not seem uniquely strange that life should continue to be given beyond the boundaries of physical death.

5

When in this life we are diminished by suffering and reduced to sterility and despair, the first sign of our resurrection is hope. It is a hope, as we saw, which is undefined. It is hope for we know not what. In retrospect we can see that the hope was inevitably without content, since it was hope for fulfilment of a kind which we could not then have imagined, let alone desired. The fulfilment of the hope was our being created into something which we could not possibly have envisaged, since it was beyond the range of our current experience. What we were given was something beyond our resources at the time, something new which was unconditioned by what we then were.

Here, however, we must make a distinction between hope and what we can call desire. Hope is hope for we know not what. It is expectancy in face of a future which is ultimately unknown. It is certainly hope of fulfilment (otherwise it would not be hope) but we have not the first idea of what that fulfilment will turn out to be. Desire, on the other hand, takes its form and outline from what we already are. And the object of desire is ourselves as already known to us with our present capacity for pleasure and joy expanded and transmogrified, but essentially the same. The object of desire is my present self with everything eliminated from it which hinders it from enjoying life. In contrast, the object of hope is a blank cheque. It is fulfilment, but the nature of that fulfilment is beyond thought and imagination. The most adequate description of hope has perhaps been given by St Paul: 'Eye hath not seen, nor ear heard, neither have entered into the heart of man, the things which God hath prepared for them that love him.'⁴ And this is something of which we have experience in this life on those occasions when we are raised from the dead. In our predicament we *desire* this or that – 'if only so and so would happen; if only x would do so and so; if only I could manage to bring off such and such a thing'. But what is fulfilled is seldom our desire, but our *hope*. Our predicament is indeed transcended and we are fulfilled, but it is in a way entirely unimagined at the time. George Eliot has given us an example of hope and its fulfilment in *Silas Marner*. In his loneliness, Silas's only consolation is his growing pile of gold. One day the gold is stolen. What he desires is to identify the thief and recover the gold. Instead, a young golden-haired child finds her way into Silas's cottage, and he grows to love her and eventually to adopt her. That is the fulfilment of his hope, and it is in a manner totally unexpected.

A great deal of our difficulty when considering the future life is that we apply to it the logic of desire instead of the logic of hope. We take it for granted that the form of our fulfilment in the future life will be modelled on what we desire as the people we are now. And this generally makes what we call heaven either ridiculous or frankly incredible or patently the projection of our own wishes on to the sky. But hope is the prospect of the radically new. It is the breaking in of what we had never even dreamed of, a fulfilment utterly beyond our power to conceive. Hence the

⁴ 1 Corinthians 2:9.

phrase 'to hope against hope', for what it really means is to hope against what is at present credible or even conceivable, to hope against desire. We know that whatever we may be able to conceive is absolutely out of the question, however much we may desire it, and yet we continue to hope. And if here on earth we have not been disappointed of our hope, if hope has not made us ashamed, what grounds can there be for limiting our expectancy to this side only of the grave? Hope is either beyond limitation or it is nothing. 'Hope implies a kind of radical refusal to reckon possibilities . . . it is as though it carried with it as a postulate the assertion that reality overflows all possible reckonings.'[5]

But this means that hope, for all its glory, requires a strict asceticism of its own, otherwise it becomes desire and may well be betrayed by the future.

Of this asceticism nobody has been a greater exemplar than the Buddha. He often seems to be totally agnostic, apparently believing nothing. Yet he expressly dissociated himself from the rational agnostic or any formal agnosticism. 'He will not have it that we can speculate even to the extent of formally expressing an agnostic position. We are not to say that we can say nothing; and this seems to me to give agnosticism a twist which completely alters its character and brings it into line with the acknowledgement of an ultimate mystery, a mystery whose ultimate and positive nature is discerned in a peculiarly incisive and modern way in this particular instance of Buddha's refusal to sanction open agnosticism.'[6] Nirvana is thus nearer to the Christian heaven than Christians generally allow. 'The same pressed lips which refused to name *conceptions* of nirvana are seen to affirm the *reality* of nirvana.'[7] The Buddha does not leave men without hope, but is careful to see that it is not hope for anything conceivable because that would be clinging to the past.

Are we very far here from St Paul's 'neither has it entered into the heart of man what God has prepared for those that love him'?[8]

---

[5] Gabriel Marcel, *Being and Having*, Dacre Press, 1949, p. 76.
[6] H. D. Lewis, in *The Study of Religions*, Penguin Books, 1969, p. 180.
[7] R. S. Slater, in ibid., p. 82 (his italics).
[8] 1 Corinthians 2:9.

Or the statement in the first epistle of St John – 'it does not yet appear what we shall be'?[9]

Such undefined hope and its fulfilment we have already experienced here now. The experience involved a break with ourselves as belonging hopelessly to the past and our being raised up to the creative call of our own future. Physical death is the last and final break with our past. We cannot prove that the miracle of resurrection will automatically follow. But we can take to heart the fact that it has invariably done so hitherto. 'Old things are passed away; behold all things are become new.'[10] We could say that God's turning to us is new and strange every morning. Those aware of that fact can hardly fail to hope.

6

If we are ready for life in the sense of being open to its power and possibilities, then we are also ready for death. If we are aware of resurrection in the present, then we shall not be over-concerned about resurrection in the future. What Jesus said about becoming as little children and taking no thought for the morrow applies with special force to our future in and beyond the grave. We live now from hour to hour, from minute to minute, as those who are ever receiving from the unknown, and that is all we need to know. Ours can be the confidence of a child living in his father's house whose needs are supplied as, and only as, they arise. Our faith cannot exist in a vacuum of speculative possibilities. Faith is evoked only by the particular situation in which it is needed. (Hence, for example, the impossibility of answering the question, 'Would I be willing to be martyred?') For faith is not a static entity which we have or haven't got or which we have in one degree and not in another. It is always coming into being. It is always being created. It is always being called forth as and when it is needed. When the occasion first arises, we feel as likely as not that our faith is too weak to begin to cope. Then slowly we discover that our faith is matched to our need. And the sign that it is so is seldom any glorious certainty or sense of uplift, but simply

[9] 1 John 3:2.   [10] 2 Corinthians 5:17.

the fact that, however much we are wounded and hurt, we are not overwhelmed after all, or perhaps better, being indeed over-whelmed, we still retain that spasmodic glimmer of hope. With regard to all the deaths we have to die, including the final death of the grave, we must always remember that sufficient unto the day is the evil thereof and that as our days are so shall our strength be. If we are like little children we shall not worry about what is going to happen next year or even tomorrow.

7

The source of our confidence cannot be defined. For our confidence is precisely faith in resurrection. And resurrection ceases to be resurrection and becomes no more than another example of human banality, a futile extravaganza, once it is pinned down in a definition. We can experience resurrection at first hand, but we have no concepts, no words, no linguistic forms, in which we can set it out with anything approaching adequacy. We are reminded of Heidegger's statement that 'what is not thought is the supreme gift that any thinking has to give'.[11]

We can approach what is meant only by reading between the lines. For resurrection is God creating, and that passes infinitely beyond the range of our conceptual or linguistic machinery. If we think we have successfully nailed resurrection to the wall, then we are worshipping an idol, and when it is shown up for what it is, we shall feel the need to rush to its defence. 'Divine truth,' on the other hand, 'is a unique kind of uncertainty. . . . It comes, if it comes at all, unexpectedly, at some moment of unknowing, exile, abandonment.'[12]

It must be understood, therefore, that what we have said in this book about resurrection is in terms only of symbols and images which can do no more than point to the reality with which they are concerned. Yet the reality itself is not far off. As our creative source it is nearer to us than we are to ourselves. And if the reality

[11] Martin Heidegger, *Was heibt Denken*, Tübingen, 1954, p. 72.
[12] E. Lampert, in A. J. Philippon (ed.), *The Orthodox Ethos*, Holywell Press, 1964, p. 226.

is ultimately indescribable, that is not only because it infinitely transcends us, but also because it encompasses us, informing everything we are as the water informs and fills the sea. For the tabernacle of God is with men as the Eternal Word continuously takes his world to himself and raises it up to resurrection and life.